Foreword

The Centre for Co-operation with European Economies in Transition, which was created in March 1990, is the focal point for co-operation between the OECD and central and eastern European countries. Its major responsibility is to design and manage a programme of policy advice and technical assistance which puts the expertise of the Secretariat and Member countries at the disposal of countries engaged in economic reform. This advice or assistance can take numerous forms, including conferences, seminars, missions and workshops in order to explore policy questions or review draft legislation; it can also include training for government officials who are called to implement market-oriented policies.

In December 1990 the OECD initiated a programme "Partners in Transition" for the purpose of providing more focused assistance to those countries that are more advanced in introducing market-oriented reforms and desire to become members of OECD. Additional activities, which the Centre would co-ordinate under this programme, could include reviews of the country's general economic situation and prospects, reviews of issues and policies in specific areas and participation in certain OECD committees.

In all these activities, the Centre maintains close relations with other multilateral bodies such as the G-24 co-ordinated by the Commission of the European Communities, the International Monetary Fund, the World Bank, the European Investment Bank, the European Bank for Reconstruction and Development, with the mutual objective of ensuring the complementarity of respective efforts to support economic reforms in Central and Eastern Europe.

Four activities in the Centre's current work programme have been designated as part of the OECD's response to the invitation of the Bonn Conference of the CSCE to host meetings of experts from CSCE participating States and OECD Member States to promote the process of economic reform.

This report is based on two seminars dealing with some of the main issues and strategies surrounding the transition of central and eastern European countries to market economies. The seminars, held on 20-21 June 1990 in Paris, were organised by the Economic and Statistics Department with the support of the Centre for Co-operation with European Economies in Transition.

These proceedings were edited by Hans J. Blommestein and Michael Marrese. Mr. Blommestein is an economist with the Economics and Statistics Department of the OECD. Mr. Marrese, a consultant to the OECD, is on leave from Northwestern University, Evanston, Illinois, USA, where he holds the position of associate professor of economics.

The report is published on the responsibility of the Secretary-General of the OECD.

Contents

Property Rights Reform: Hungarian Country Study

by *K. Crane*

Strategies for Economic Transformation in central and eastern Europe: Role of Financial Market Reform

by *L. Brainard*

Structural Conditions for a Stable Monetary Régime and Efficient Allocation of Investment: Soviet Country Study

by *W. Schrettl*

Foreword

This volume is the second in a series of publications by the OECD Centre for Co-operation with European Economies in Transition. The purpose of this book, and those which will follow, is to add to understanding of the problems which the central and eastern European countries are, or will be, facing as they move from a centrally-planned to a market-oriented economy. The transformation of these economic systems is by both its nature and scale a task and an effort without precedent in our economic history. The lack of an adequate body of knowledge, from which governments can draw guidance, makes the transition all the more difficult, while the conditions of economic distress that characterise these countries at the beginning of the process make it all the more urgent. The co-operation and assistance of the prosperous market economies of the "West" could be crucial in avoiding such a transformation succumbing to the many difficulties.

Since late 1989, these reforming countries have been addressing requests for advice, co-operation and assistance to the OECD. The long history of the Organisation in supporting the development of market economies is one of the reasons for such requests. The OECD embodies, and perpetuates, the success of the co-operative experience of its predecessor, the Organisation for European Economic Co-operation (OEEC), established in 1948 to bolster the efforts of Western European countries in rebuilding their economies. In this endeavour a key factor was the support, through the Marshall Plan, of the United States of America.

The wealth of experience and expertise which the OECD and its Member countries can put at the disposal of the reforming countries in central and eastern Europe is considerable, covering as it does all the domains of economics as well as their interlinkages. Thus, the potential contribution of the OECD to the reform of those economies is unique.

In order to enable it to meet the growing number of requests by these countries, the OECD created, in March 1990, the Centre for Co-operation with the European Economies in Transition. The purpose of the Centre is to provide technical advice, to undertake policy dialogue and, in a few cases, to train officials in the context of a programme of activities that is designed and reviewed annually. The Centre is not established as a separate agency within the OECD but rather as an infrastructure that can rely on and mobilise the know-how both of the OECD staff and of its Member countries. Technical advice and policy dialogue take numerous forms and cover a wide range of subjects, spanning from macroeconomic issues to structural problems. Seminars, workshops and technical meetings are being held, involving on one side the OECD Secretariat, together with experts and policymakers from OECD countries, and on the other side, policymakers, officials and experts from central and

9

eastern Europe. The experience of the business community is also called upon where appropriate. Specific policy questions are explored or draft legislation and administrative practices are reviewed. Furthermore, analyses of some economic sectors are being conducted in those countries. Training of government officials involved in implementing market-oriented policies is being carried out on a limited scale, for example in areas such as competition policy. In implementing its programme, the Centre maintains close relations with other multilateral institutions such as the International Monetary Fund, the World Bank and the EEC Commission, as well as with other multilateral programmes such as the G-24 programme that is co-ordinated by the EEC Commission.

The Centre's commitment to all these activities has been enhanced with the adoption of special programmes for co-operation in the context of the initiative "Partners in Transition" which was launched in December 1990. This initiative focuses on those countries in economic transition that are more advanced in the introduction of economic and social reforms and have expressed the intention of becoming members of the OECD. Each of these programmes is oriented towards the specific reform needs of a "partner in transition", and can also include the participation of these countries as an observer in the activities of certain OECD committees.

First steps in launching the Centre's activities must be to assess the extent and characteristics of the needs of the reforming economies, to understand what are the most appropriate instruments for support, and to establish the contribution being furnished by other institutions. As one means to this end, the Centre is sponsoring four major conferences. Each provides an opportunity to examine, with the representatives of the reforming countries, a specific set of issues in order to identify priorities for action and for international assistance in the transition to a market-based economy. These priorities can be expected to constitute the basis for developing specific activities which may be of interest to one or several of these countries. These conferences have also been designed as part of the OECD response to the invitation of the Bonn meeting of the Conference on Security and Co-operation in Europe to host meetings of experts from the CSCE participating States and OECD Member States to promote the process of economic reform.

The first conference was held in September 1990 and dealt with the problem of reforming the statistical systems. The second conference, in November 1990, focused on the problems and difficulties of managing the economy in the transition to a market-system. The seminar, whose proceedings are reported in this volume, was organised in preparation for this conference and was held in June 1990. The third conference, in January 1991, was devoted to the issues of tax reform, while the last conference of this cycle, in the summer of 1991, will examine the creation of a labour market and the social implications of the systemic reforms in central and eastern Europe.

Salvatore Zecchini
Director of the Centre for Co-operation
with the European Economies in Transition

Centrally Planned Economies in Transition:
an Introductory Overview of Selected Issues and Strategies

Hans J. Blommestein, Michael Marrese and Salvatore Zecchini

Background

The transformation of a centrally planned economy (CPE) into a market economy never occurred in the pre-perestroika era[1]. Economic theory offered little guidance on how to replace central planning with the market. However, the liberating political upheavals of 1989 in central and eastern Europe and the Soviet Union have made the transition from CPE to market economy one of the priorities of the 1990s. Moreover, these countries' early experience with economic perestroika has demonstrated that costly and time-consuming debates over property rights, political institutions, market-oriented "rules of the game", financial infrastructure, macroeconomic policy, and the social safety net are inevitable components of this transformation process[2].

Against this background the Economics and Statistics Department of the OECD, with the support of the Centre for Co-Operation with the European Economies in Transition, held two successive seminars on 20-21 June 1990 entitled:

a) Day One: "Property Rights Reform and its Impact on Macroeconomic Performance and Social Welfare Needs";
b) Day Two: "The Structural Conditions for a Stable Macroeconomic Regime and Efficient Allocation of Investment".

The five papers that were presented at these seminars are published in this volume in the order of their appearance. This introductory chapter presents the main ideas of the five principal contributors, the other seminar participants, and ourselves on why, how, and when private property, competition, sound monetary and fiscal policy, price liberalisation, enterprise incentives and financial infrastructure enter into the transformation process.

Of course, other elements – not directly addressed in this study – also will be essential for the success of the transformation process. Among these are well-functioning markets for all factors of production, a legal system that permits and protects varied forms of ownership and market transactions, and an effective government

The authors would like to thank: **Paul Atkinson, Alexandra Bibbee, Grant Kirkpatrick** and **George McDowell** for their helpful comments and suggestions.

bound by "the rule of law" and responsible for public goods, externalities, and the social safety net.

Sections 2 and 3 of this chapter focus on the first day's topic by examining the importance of private property and competition to former CPEs and by summarising the papers by Jozef M. van Brabant, Keith Crane, and D. Mario Nuti. Sections 4 and 5 cover the second day's ideas by focusing on the objectives of macroeconomic policy during the transition period and by summarising the papers by Lawrence J. Brainard and Wolfram Schrettl. In Section 6, the general spirit of the seminars is discussed, while conclusions appear in Section 7.

Property rights reform and the creation of competitive markets

The growing inadequacy of the extensive growth strategy and the structural problems associated with central planning were the major impetus behind pre-perestroika economic reform efforts. In almost all CPEs this meant the search for the optimal degree of decentralisation in economies which continued to be based primarily on social ownership of the means of production[3]. In any event, decentralisation of decision-making (including the introduction of self-managed enterprises) turned out to be a very poor substitute for the creation of a market economy. Growth and efficiency did not increase. Soft-budget constraints were not hardened and in many cases financial discipline among enterprises even deteriorated. Moreover, decentralisation led to even more bureaucratic bargaining between ministries and enterprises about preferential access to credits and foreign exchange, special subsidies, discretionary taxation, and so forth.

The failure of these pre-perestroika reform efforts helped many policy makers in the CPEs to realise that the creation of a full-fledged market economy was necessary. In addition, other factors caused these policy makers to believe that rapid and large-scale privatisation of state firms, together with the removal of obstacles to entry for new private enterprises, should form an integral part of any transformation strategy.

First, former CPEs need to increase economic efficiency on a durable basis. Privatisation based on clearly defined and legally recognised property rights would contribute to increased efficiency by replacing bureaucratic incentives with profit-oriented ones. Even under the current market structures, this would lead to more mobility in both labour and capital, and to improvements in the collection and utilisation of demand and supply information. Under more competitive market structures, privatisation coupled with appropriate incentives would also promote a general increase in the effort of workers and managers to improve organisational and technological conditions[4].

A second major reason for a radical change in property rights concerns its structural contribution to macroeconomic stability. Selling or leasing state-owned enterprises helps to eliminate the monetary overhang. In addition, the long-term maintenance of sound macroeconomic policies will be difficult without large-scale and rapid privatisation of state-owned enterprises because the government is unlikely to be able to enforce financial discipline if state-owned enterprises remain a dominant part of the economy.

12

Unfortunately these compelling reasons for privatisation have not reduced the controversy about the process. The issue of whether and "how to privatise" is explosive because it involves transfers of wealth and is likely to clash with social perceptions about "what is fair". Consequently, proposals to sell state-owned enterprises to workers, managers or foreigners, or to give away such enterprises are hotly debated.

Another reason for the delay in privatisation concerns disagreements about whether to break up monopolies before or after privatisation. One group of economists argues that demonopolisation before divestiture is absolutely essential because lack of competition is a dominant feature of the former CPEs. Otherwise, privatisation would result in an economy dominated by private monopolies. The other group offers three reasons why monopoly power may be resolved relatively easily once privatisation has occurred. First, a "free-entry promoting" change in the regulatory environment could reduce existing monopoly power. Second, open regimes for international trade and foreign direct investment may be very effective mechanisms for quickly generating competition. Third, privatisation combined with or preceded by price deregulation may quickly attract new entrants thereby squeezing "windfall" and "monopoly" profits. Nonetheless, even the latter group of economists concedes that for large state-owned enterprises operating as natural or network monopolies, it may be necessary that the government get the regulatory environment right before privatisation[5].

Four technical factors constitute the final explanation of the slow pace of privatisation. First, policy makers and the public in former CPEs do not possess a clear idea of how capital markets operate and are unfamiliar with the fact that in a market economy "an enterprise's asset value as measured by the market value of its stock may fluctuate widely due to any shock that influences the expected profit stream of that enterprise". This is mostly because the absence of financial markets in these countries has meant that the value of state-owned enterprises has not been influenced by changes in prices, technology, new entrants and wealth. This unfamiliarity in how assets are valued has produced an unrealistic belief that an *ex ante* fair privatisation process can be constructed. Second, even if decision makers in former CPEs fully understood how capital markets operate, privatisation is controversial because there are difficulties in establishing reservation prices (prices below which the state should not sell) since enterprises have not functioned in a market economy, have not faced serious competitive pressure and have not been audited in an economically meaningful manner. Third, some segments of society perceive privatisation to be a "process of selling the country to foreigners" because the stock of accumulated "savings" of households and enterprises is small relative to the "value" of assets to be privatised. Fourth and most important, privatisation can occur only after the following information is known: the constraints on ownership rights (for example, commitments to retrain employees before they are released from their jobs), who owns enterprises to be privatised, and who is responsible for previously accumulated enterprise debt and environmental damage.

In other words, time- and resource-consuming coalition building characterises the privatisation of state-owned enterprises because many potential combinations of people could benefit and there is no clear-cut economic rationale for picking one set of beneficiaries over another. Moreover, analytical considerations and practical experience in both former CPEs and market economies indicate that there is no single "best" scheme for privatisation. Also, with respect to the process of divestiture itself, there is no unique optimal strategy. Thus privatisation should be guided by transpar-

ent procedures that may differ according to: type of asset involved (apartment, farm land, small retail outlet or large industrial firm) and the extent to which the "asset to be privatised" needs new capital, managerial skill, and technological expertise[6].

Overview of the papers on property rights reform

Jozef M. van Brabant, in his paper "Property Rights' Reform, Macroeconomic Performance, and Welfare", starts by noting the enthusiasm of former CPEs for creating markets, including capital markets. These markets are responsible for allocating existing capital, creating new capital, and stimulating entry and exit. If the tasks of capital markets are to be carried out successfully, property rights must be: well-defined and well-protected, placed in the hands of those with purely economic responsibilities, and enforced by neutral regulators in conjunction with an effective judicial system.

Brabant then argues that defining privatisation as asset sales is too limiting. Rather, privatisation should be seen as a transfer from the public to the private sector of rights to residual enterprise income. This transfer affects an enterprise's incentive structure and therefore its performance. Brabant goes on to note that ownership, competition and the regulatory environment are interrelated influences on allocative efficiency. However, the latter two factors, Brabant emphasises, have a larger effect on performance than ownership *per se*.

Privatisation is desirable, Brabant contends, because socialism has failed, the bureaucratic power of the Communist Party and government apparatus must be destroyed, and competition must be promoted. Yet privatisation should not be characterised only as state firms becoming private firms. It may also take the form of leasing enterprises to the highest bidder or properly monitoring enterprises that remain state-owned yet operate under much more stimulating incentive structures than existed previously. Brabant goes on to argue that reduction in the monopoly power of large-scale enterprises is imperative under all forms of privatisation and should certainly occur before the ownership of large-scale state-owned enterprises is transferred into private hands.

Despite the desirability of privatising state assets in former CPEs, Brabant emphasises that the difficulties are enormous. For example, the selling or leasing of state-owned assets requires proper pricing. However, proper pricing is hard to accomplish given the absence of capital markets, the tiny size of the private sector, the controversy over selling assets to foreigners, the thin layer of domestic entrepreneurs, non-uniform accounting rules among state-owned enterprises, and confusion over who is the legal owner of existing state-owned assets.

As a result, Brabant discusses alternative methods of privatisation from organisational, efficiency, and equity points of view. He begins with spontaneous privatisation, which is the transformation of a state-owned enterprise into a joint-stock company, whose new owners are often the enterprise's former managers. Then he describes means of distributing assets free of charge, allocating user rights via leasing arrangements and management contracts, and selling assets.

14

He concludes with an implicit sequence for the privatisation process:

First:
- all "state-owned" assets should be re-nationalised to establish clear legal property rights;
- housing, handicrafts, and small businesses should be privatised through bidding procedures;
- land reform should be undertaken;
- almost all state-owned enterprises should be turned into professionally monitored joint-stock companies;

Second:
- the government should promote competitive behaviour by creating an appropriate institutional environment and performance-enhancing incentive schemes;
- the government should pursue comprehensive stabilisation, enact fiscal reform, demonopolise, and liberalise prices;

Third:
- once state-owned enterprises are behaving like competitive firms, their outright sale to the public should occur at a measured pace.

Keith Crane, in his paper "Property Rights Reform: Hungarian Case Study", addresses three questions. First, what are the economic reasons for the privatisation of state-owned industries in Hungary? Crane cites four types of evidence in favour of a clearly articulated government approach to privatisation.

- There is overwhelming proof that Hungarian state-owned industry has used and invested capital much less efficiently than private industry in market economies.
- Substantial evidence demonstrates that the Hungarian Government has been inept in choosing where to allocate investment funds.
- Hungarian managers of state-owned enterprises have faced institutional incentives that have caused them to use existing capital stock less efficiently than their Western counterparts.
- The well-publicised attempts by enterprise managers and former Communist Party officials to buy state enterprises at bargain prices have inflamed public outrage. Therefore, the state should act quickly to dispose of state-owned assets in an open and orderly manner in order to prevent the spontaneous privatisation that so upsets the population.

Second, Crane comments on how privatisation is likely to be carried out. He begins with a description of the legal and institutional framework for privatisation that the Hungarians have already put into place. Crane then describes three trends: large state enterprises have been sold in order to obtain a "fair" value as judged by an outside appraiser and as determined by a widely publicised auction; a substantial number of small manufacturing plants, workshops, wholesale operations, and retail outlets have been spontaneously privatised; and state-owned housing has been sold to tenants at favourable prices. He next discusses new proposals to privatise the remaining medium and large enterprises. These include: reverse discrimination against state-owned enterprises; giving or selling state-owned enterprises to non-profit Hungarian institutions; and the sale of enterprise shares to current employees. Finally, Crane describes the complexities behind the privatisation of land, the political debate over the pace of privatisation, and the Hungarian Government's restrictions on foreign ownership.

Third, given the unavailability of official statistical data about the Hungarian private sector, Crane uses information from the Hungarian press to assess the initial economic effects of several types of privatisation. Crane begins by focusing on foreign investment – the type of privatisation for which there is the most data. Foreign investment was valued at $833 million as of June 1989. The associated in-flow was much less than government officials had anticipated. In any case, the following tendencies have held:

- Hungarian enterprises have sought foreign investors actively, partly to avoid bankruptcy or loss of competitiveness.
- Foreign involvement has typically produced: dramatic reductions in management and in the workforce, increased profitability, improved labour productivity, better wages for remaining employees, an infusion of new capital, and superior access to new technology.

Another form of Hungarian privatisation has been the spontaneous type initiated by former managers of state enterprises. In most of these instances, former managers have retained their jobs and have taken an ownership position in the new firm. Here there has been less evidence of improved productivity, although a few success stories have emerged.

This process of spontaneous privatisation in Hungary has created a backlash against privatisation because the majority of Hungarian citizens perceive this process as tainted by fraud. Why should previously unsuccessful enterprise managers profit immensely from their efforts to sell state enterprises to themselves at bargain prices without open bidding?

Crane then puts forward three problems associated with privatisation which although not yet observed are theoretically plausible. To begin, government tax revenue could decline as enterprises move from state to private ownership because fully effective tax collection of private-sector income has not yet been established. Next, if the Hungarian Government places a high priority on preserving current jobs, this will mean continued government subsidisation of poorly performing enterprises at the expense of heavy taxation of well-functioning enterprises. Such profit-levelling could slow down the privatisation process. Finally, legal suits have already been initiated by former owners of what is now state property. If such litigation becomes commonplace, it will impede the process of privatisation.

Crane concludes by noting that privatisation involving foreign investors has produced many improvements in enterprise performance. The record is less clear when privatisation has only involved Hungarians. Nonetheless, the process has been slower than anticipated due to the reluctance of foreign investors to enter the Hungarian market and the substantial scepticism within Hungary about the manner in which privatisation has been conducted.

D. Mario Nuti, in his paper "Privatisation of Socialist Economies: General Issues and the Polish Case", explores five arguments in favour of the "sale, gift or rental of state assets to private individuals or companies" in central and eastern Europe. First, both world-wide experience with privatisation and the principal-agent literature suggest that privatisation alters incentives in a manner that raises the efficiency of enterprises. For instance, managers of private enterprises in a country with developed capital markets are subject to: contractual discipline imposed by shareholders, take-over discipline enforced by potential bidders, and bankruptcy discipline initiated by creditors. Managers of state enterprises face no such pressures to promote efficiency.

Second, the need to replace bureaucratic inertia with decentralised vitality, the need to weaken the opportunity for political interference in economic life, and the need to harden enterprise budget constraints are three system-specific arguments in favour of privatisation in central and eastern Europe.

Third, private ownership was not completely eradicated in socialist economies. In fact, wherever private ownership was present, there always was built-in pressure for its expansion. Nuti argues that private property is superfluous only in a utopian society in which scarcity is absent. Otherwise, there will be popular demand for the legalisation of private property.

Fourth, once a limited scope for property rights is established, there are efficiency reasons for their extension to full-fledged capitalism. For instance, if a person is allowed to save, why shouldn't that person allocate a portion of savings to profitable investment projects? If a person is allowed to hold an equity position in an enterprise, why shouldn't that person be allowed to establish and run his own enterprise?

Fifth, Nuti sees no natural point in the development of an economy at which to restrict the further spread of capitalism. However, he admits that it might be possible to stimulate entrepreneurship under limited property rights (say municipal or co-operative ownership) if appropriate incentive schemes can be created.

Nuti provides three suggestions for the implementation of privatisation in socialist economies:
- Property rights of all state assets should be transferred to a single public organisation before privatisation takes place. This may mean that employees of self-managed firms may need to receive compensation for giving up their property rights.
- Privatisation via free distribution of shares of state enterprises to the population is counterproductive because it would increase consumer demand and worsen inflationary pressure. Spontaneous privatisation is even worse than free distribution of shares because it is inflationary and is perceived by the population as being a fraudulent process.
- The sale of shares in state enterprises should occur after stabilisation and fiscal reform have been implemented. This sequence would minimise the extent to which state assets are sold at prices offensive to the population.

As background to his final section on recent privatisation in Poland, Nuti reviews Poland's earlier fall in real output and per capita consumption, accumulation of external debt, and hyper-inflation. During this disheartening pre-perestroika period, many people in Poland moved from the state sector to the private sector. Indeed, in 1988 employment in the private sector was almost one-third of all employment and was growing rapidly while state employment was declining.

Nuti then discusses the Mazowiecki Government's introduction of the following stabilisation package on 1 January 1990: abolition of government subsidies; a sharp reduction in the government's budget deficit; monetary discipline; positive real interest rates; almost complete price liberalisation; very mild wage indexation; and internal convertibility of the zloty.

One might expect that the combination of the above three elements – a society relatively familiar with the private sector, a market-oriented and relatively stable macroeconomic environment, and an underutilised and hungry population – would lead to rapid, successful privatisation. Nuti goes on to show that this has not been the case.

Nuti sees two factors as being responsible for a paralysis of the privatisation process in Poland. First, self-management was incorporated into Polish state enterprises in 1981. Since then Polish workers have had rights over: managerial appointments and dismissals, evaluation of the enterprise's current performance, distribution of profit, and investment decision making. In a private enterprise, stockholders usually have those rights. Thus if privatisation is going to move forward in Poland, Polish workers need to be compensated for their loss of self-management rights (perhaps by being awarded shares in the newly privatised company).

Second, there is no single rule for compensating workers that is perceived to be fair. Indeed, many tough questions need to be addressed in order to deal with transforming state enterprises into private ones. How many shares of a company should workers receive? Should workers in different companies be awarded the same percentage of share ownership even though capital-labour ratios among companies vary widely? Why should workers in self-managed enterprises be the only ones given shares in the state sector? What compensation should be given to employees in the government service sector, to the unemployed, and to those in the private sector?

The latest Polish Government response to the privatisation puzzle is incorporated in the July 1990 law on privatisation and involves:
- The establishment of a Ministry of Property Transformation that is to supervise the transformation of state enterprises into share companies. The Treasury will initially be the single shareholder in these companies.
- Within two years, the Treasury will sell its shares to domestic and foreign investors. However, 20 per cent of shares will be reserved for enterprise workers at a maximum 50 per cent discount. Also, there will be an overall ceiling of 10 per cent on foreign ownership of a particular enterprise.

Certainly some new initiatives on the Polish Government's part are needed. As of March 1990, only $200 million of foreign capital was invested in Poland – far less than in Hungary. In fact, Nuti's paper provides evidence that the privatisation process in Poland up until now has been dominated by the growth of private enterprises and the withering away of state enterprises rather than by a transformation scheme.

The objectives of macroeconomic policy during the transition period

The first objective of macroeconomic management during the transition period is to eliminate or reduce chronic excess demand and inflationary pressure. This involves not only the eradication of the so-called "monetary overhang" but also the removal of the flow causes of chronic excess demand by restoring financial discipline at the enterprise level; reducing budget deficits; and tightening monetary policy. The second objective is partly related to the first one because it concerns the implementation of effective macroeconomic austerity policies. This in turn requires the introduction of more effective instruments for macroeconomic control. On the fiscal side, reform means the introduction of a new tax and subsidy system characterised by stable and uniform rates, such as the value-added tax. On the monetary side, reform involves: the shift of financial intermediation from the budget to the banking system, the establishment of an independent central bank, and the introduction of a decentralised banking system similar to those in OECD countries.

This second objective is particularly difficult to attain because as soon as the market-oriented transformation creates privately-owned enterprises, the central authorities lose their capacity to suppress macroeconomic imbalances through traditional administrative measures. The following two examples illustrate the problem. First, the traditional tax collection mechanism breaks down as the government's tax base – the surpluses of state-owned enterprises – erodes when enterprises are transferred to the private sector or when newly organised non-state economic activity takes "profit" away from state-owned enterprises. Second, if the traditional monetary system serving enterprises continues to ignore profit-oriented criteria after enterprises have become more autonomous, then net domestic credit to enterprises could grow at an unprecedented rate. Therefore, a critical challenge for the authorities is to develop a set of indirect instruments for effective macroeconomic control before or in parallel with the changes on the micro-economic level.

The third objective of macroeconomic management is to minimise price instability in the initial stages of the transformation. In this regard, Wolf (1990) notes that the critical issue is whether the imposition of financial discipline and more competition have effectively preceded, or at least occurred simultaneously with, the decontrol of prices and wages. This of course involves the elimination of the flow causes of excess demand and the creation of effective instruments for macroeconomic control before prices and wages are fully decontrolled.

Overview of the papers on the structural conditions for a stable macroeconomic regime

Lawrence J. Brainard addresses three questions in his paper "Strategies for Economic Reform in Central and Eastern Europe: The Role of Financial Market Reform". What is the fundamental goal of the transformation process and how does financial market reform contribute to achieving that goal? Where do efforts to reform East European economies stand today? Which new perspectives on financial reform are most promising?

To Brainard, the goal of the transformation process should be sustained growth under conditions of stable prices. This requires the creation of an effective market for capital, which would impose financial discipline on enterprises. If financial discipline is to be attained, three reforms must be introduced simultaneously. First, enterprises need to be restructured in the sense of being: faced with market prices, hard budget constraints, and uniform accounting and supervisory practices; freed from any previ-

19

ously accumulated yet unrepayable debts through either bankruptcy or rehabilitation; and allowed to make input and output choices. Some will be privatised, others will remain state property. Both private and state firms should be expected to be profitable in order to survive. Second, restructured state firms should be offered for sale at prices established by, for example, auctions. Third, the banking system needs to be reformed so that: profit-oriented commercial banks evaluate alternative enterprise investment proposals; the central bank controls the money supply; the central bank and other supervisory agencies monitor the behaviour of commercial banks and credit institutions.

Before analysing the current status of reform in central and eastern Europe, Brainard notes that earlier reform efforts have failed not only because of irrational relative prices and subsidies to loss-making enterprises, but also due to serious structural imbalances caused by the banking system. Redistribution of resources via allocation of loans at negative real interest rates, the refinancing of loans enterprises will never be able to service, and inadequate accounting and supervisory practices have been three long-standing distortions within the banking system.

The Polish economic programme introduced on 1 January 1990 is first reviewed. This programme consists primarily of the following economic stabilisation measures:
- a balanced fiscal budget, tight credit ceilings, and restrictive wage regulation in state enterprises;
- market-clearing price formation;
- removal of bureaucratic restrictions on the private sector;
- internal convertibility of the zloty, increasing competitive pressures on Polish enterprises.

A phased introduction of structural changes is to follow these stabilisation measures.

Brainard is critical of the Polish approach to reform because the Poles, have thus far neglected structural reform of labour and capital markets. For instance, nothing has been done to: encourage banks to make sound loans; relieve newly established state-owned commercial banks of the bad loans they inherited from the central bank; give commercial banks the right and incentive to force loss-making enterprises into bankruptcy; and form institutions which will monitor the activities of commercial banks.

In general, Brainard believes it is a mistake to undertake radical economic stabilisation until key structural reforms are ready to be implemented. For capital markets, this means that central and eastern European governments need to go beyond the current policy of eliminating firm-specific subsidies and allocating credit at market-clearing interest rates and begin to restructure the balance sheets of enterprises and banks. Thus the unrealised balance sheet losses of enterprises and banks should be allocated among employees, creditors, and society at large. For enterprises, bankruptcy, rehabilitation of viable enterprises, and privatisation are ways in which balance sheet losses can be distributed. Commercial banks should be recapitalised through removal of bad loans from their portfolios and by providing a means of raising new capital. Without recapitalisation of commercial banks, Brainard warns, it will be almost impossible to create a well-functioning capital market and to control monetary activity.

20

Brainard realises that his proposal for restructuring the balance sheets of enterprises and banks will be very costly. The government, via budgetary expenditures, will be called upon to pay unemployment benefits and to inject additional funds into both enterprises and banks. The net effect, according to Brainard, is that the government is unlikely to realise positive budgetary income from the sale of enterprises once the cost of writing off loans to enterprises is taken into account.

International agencies and Western governments could greatly assist central and eastern European countries in their banking reforms through a combination of loans, technical assistance and direct aid. If Western government assistance is insufficient, Brainard advises East European governments to hire Western experts to help introduce bank reform.

Finally, in order to point out problems other former CPEs may face, Brainard discusses the April-August 1990 change to eastern Germany's (German Democratic Republic before the unification of Germany) banking system. In April, all commercial accounts from eastern Germany's central bank were transferred to the newly created Kreditbank. The Kreditbank then contributed all of its branch offices and transferred almost all its personnel to joint ventures with two western German (Federal Republic of Germany before the unification of Germany) commercial banks. Kreditbank was left with all commercial loans from eastern Germany – no attempt was made to distinguish good from bad loans.

Since no incentive structure was established to encourage capable eastern German enterprises to repay their loans, the temptation to default was strong. The Bonn Government recognised this and, in August, announced a one-year moratorium on the servicing of this corporate debt. However, the problems do not stop there. No Western-style enterprise audits were conducted on enterprises in eastern Germany. The ownership of enterprise assets was not clarified. Both these factors have hampered the two joint-venture banks from making new loans to enterprises in eastern Germany.

Another problem encountered was the shortage of skilled banking personnel in eastern Germany. In response, the western German joint venture partners transferred 1 600 employees to branches in eastern Germany, both to manage everyday affairs and to train employees in these new branches.

The overall message of Brainard's paper is clear: banking reform is very expensive precisely because it requires enterprises to be restructured. Absorbing these costs should be done today, not tomorrow.

Wolfram Schrettl, in his paper "Structural Conditions for a Stable Monetary Regime and Efficient Allocation of Investment: Soviet Union Country Study", observes that because the Soviet economic situation has deteriorated so dramatically and is expected to deteriorate further, a quick and possibly dirty reform is the Soviet Union's only sensible alternative. Moreover, Schrettl views rapid transformation to a competitive capitalist democracy as the only way for the Soviet Union to combat corruption that allocation of resources by non-owners breeds. In addition, opponents of a switch to a market economy can exploit the "optimal sequencing debate" to delay the transformation process. Thus Schrettl argues that the debate over optimal sequencing is wasting time. Rather, following the Polish and eastern German examples, reform should be characterised by: speedy implementation of individual measures, reduction of the time-intervals between the individual measures, rapid correction of policy mistakes, and "doing well whatever is being done."

Schrettl supports his view by criticising both the Polish and Soviet approaches to reform. The radical price liberalisation and restrictive monetary and fiscal policies in Poland have eliminated the monetary overhang, but the supply response has been minimal because of the slow pace of privatisation, inattention to commercial bank reform, and failure to attract foreign capital. However, on the positive side, state enterprises have mostly been responsible for price increases, so once privatisation occurs, private firms may well drive prices down. Moreover, the combination of price liberalisation and anti-inflationary (relatively speaking) macroeconomic policies exerted pressure on the government to continue the transformation process in order to bring the economy out of recession. In the Soviet case, privatisation, de-monopolisation, and other institutional reforms may be implemented before price liberalisation is initiated. So while the monetary overhang may be reduced by selling stock in newly formed companies, many prices will still be non-market clearing, thus queues and arbitrage opportunities will abound. In addition, privatisation is very time consuming. These considerations lead Schrettl to a message similar to Brainard's: stabilisation and institutional reform should be enacted together.

Schrettl goes on to focus on the conditions necessary for the creation of an effective two-level banking system – a central bank empowered to conduct an independent monetary policy and commercial banks that compete for deposits and loans. Modernisation of the Soviet central bank will require technical assistance in the areas of: banking supervision, money markets, short-term securities, payments schemes, foreign-exchange operations, internal accounting and auditing procedures, and so forth. The IMF is co-ordinating assistance from many Western central banks to the Polish central bank, and similar assistance could be organised for the Soviet Gosbank. Yet even if Western central banks are willing to engage in such assistance, two problems remain: the Soviets do not as yet have enough trained personnel to operate a Western-type central bank, and it may be difficult for Gosbank to establish credibility. As a result, Schrettl sees a need for international banks and Western commercial banks to, on a large scale, lend Gosbank their personnel and train Gosbank's own staff. He also hopes that an early decision in favour of an independent Gosbank will signal a serious commitment to monetary stability.

Relatively "easy-to-implement" conditions for independent commercial banks include: removal of sectoral restrictions for existing commercial banks and formation of new banks; and introduction of uniform accounting standards and market-oriented methods of compiling balance-sheets. However, other requirements are more difficult to establish: market-clearing prices so that the assets of Soviet banks can be meaningfully evaluated; availability of technically trained personnel (perhaps ten thousand Western bank staff would need to work in the Soviet Union for several years); development of expertise in judging the creditworthiness of investment proposals; recapitalisation of existing commercial banks and enterprises; and clarification of ownership rights over firms and land.

Schrettl is well aware that financial reform *per se* would be ineffective unless other "environmental" conditions are supportive of sensible banking practice. He concludes his article by advocating: a sharp increase in the net worth of individuals and enterprises so that they have collateral on which to borrow; privatisation of state assets so that newly formed private enterprises will have less incentive to extend inter-enterprise credit; and establishment of markets for money and capital. Schrettl does not believe full convertibility should be a first priority, although he discusses the many difficulties with limited convertibility.

Overview of the seminars

People's expectations have a major impact on the economic transformation of their country. Expectations themselves are a function of beliefs, goals, and experience. In the seminars, the peoples and governments of central and eastern Europe and the Soviet Union were portrayed as having a strong belief that democracy, markets, and integration into the world economy should replace their previous political-economic systems. It was also pointed out that central and eastern Europeans and Soviets have been worried about who will survive and eventually prosper from the transformation. In addition, they have shown distrust in their governments' ability to make sound economic decisions. So while popular beliefs have been opposed to a continuation of the old system, the leaderships in these countries have not succeeded in convincing people that the transformation process will improve their lives. This initial scepticism is partly due to the negative early results of the transformation policy – substantial price increases but modest supply responses.

Among seminar participants, there was a great deal of agreement concerning the goals of the economies in transition: property rights reform, substantial privatisation, price reform, macro policies that are anti-inflationary, banking and financial reform, competition policy, regulatory restructuring and creation of social safety nets. Yet the transforming economies do not know exactly what sort of Western model they should follow. Can Czechoslovakia seriously contemplate turning into another Sweden; do Poland and Hungary want to follow the example of Hong Kong or Great Britain?

The participants felt that ambiguity over the final destination of the transformation process has been a minor problem compared to the inertia that has been haunting Bulgaria, Czechoslovakia, Hungary, Romania, and the Soviet Union. This inertia has prevented these economies from taking advantage of the following policies that would have improved the expectations of both the general public and foreign investors:

- adherence to non-inflationary policies (in some cases, only after the monetary overhang has been eliminated);
- rapid implementation of the relatively non-controversial privatisation of apartments, and small businesses;
- development of a social safety net;
- immediate attention to price reform and institutional reform in areas that are likely to create the least resistance and to yield visible pay-offs (agriculture, energy, retail trade, banking, and foreign trade).

A debate arose over the reasons behind this inertia. Certainly some caution is warranted when issues such as one's future position in society, general economic opportunities, equity, sovereignty, and the involvement of foreigners in one's country are at stake. On the other hand, the direction is clear: away from the old system toward a full-fledged market economy. The debate then is not about direction – any thoughts of a third way have been forgotten – but about the sequencing of policies.

The Seminar participants were split over the wisdom of worrying about optimal sequencing. Some felt that the debate over sequencing has been a time-consuming academic exercise that has not produced better policy selection. These economists stressed the need for decisive, sensible leadership rather than for public debate over sequencing. Political leaders via their actions need to convince their people that the goals of the transformation are attractive enough to justify the costs. In general terms, the short-term goals are survival, fairness, and active participation in the economic transformation which can be met by ensuring a minimal living standard, creating efficient factor markets, and promoting new laws and regulatory bodies that encourage private ownership and competition. The long-term goals are economic prosperity and democracy. Most strategies to promote these long-term goals should include encouragement of entrepreneurial activity, institutional reform, and laws that foster foreign investment but discourage foreign exploitation. Thus, the action-oriented economists believe that there is no magic formula for the transformation, but rather many plausible strategies, one of which should be adopted as quickly as possible.

Supporters of the sequencing debate see existing transformation strategies as being incomplete and fear that hasty action may not be fortuitous. Debate over sequencing, they claim, should be fostered in order to prevent governments from making serious errors.

This description of the debate may be sharper than the actual policy advice offered by both groups. For instance, most participants agreed that:

  - A major boost in entrepreneurial activity requires privatisation of some state-owned assets, foreign investment, and the development of capital markets.
  - High-quality management requires the incentives inherent in privatisation and training in Western countries, joint ventures, or management institutes.
  - Well-functioning labour markets require skill-specific incentives, job placement services, and retraining centres.
  - Well-functioning capital markets require banking reform, creation of new financial institutions, establishment of regulatory agencies, and the participation of privately-operated enterprises.

More specifically, the following two rules and three-stage sequence may be taken as representative of the discussion:

Rule 1. Each stage should embody as much simultaneity as popular forbearance, budgetary restrictions, skilled labour constraints, and foreign-exchange considerations allow.

Rule 2. Each stage should follow the previous stage as quickly as the above-mentioned constraints allow.

Stage 1:
  - a timetable for the entire transformation process;
  - monetary, tax and expenditure policies that are consistent with macroeconomic stability (this includes the creation of market-oriented macroeconomic policy instruments);
  - market-clearing price liberalisation;
  - de-monopolisation and an expanded role for competitive imports;
  - the privatisation of most homes and small businesses;
  - a social safety net including job retraining programmes;
  - banking reform and enterprise restructuring;

- institutions to regulate financial markets, the privatisation process, foreign investment, and the newly "freed" enterprises;
- initial liberalisation of foreign trade (limited currency auctions, movement toward uniform incentives across sectors and trade partners, and direct access for enterprises to export and import possibilities).

Stage 2:
- correction of Stage 1 mistakes;
- readjustment of the transformation timetable;
- the completion of the price reform;
- implementation of internal currency convertibility;
- the large-scale privatisation of medium and large state-owned enterprises;
- the formation of stock and bond markets;
- enlargement of the role that foreign enterprises and foreign banks have in the economy;
- a continuation of regulatory and institutional reform; and
- further liberalisation of trade.

Stage 3:
- the completion of the processes begun in stages one and two;
- implementation of external currency convertibility; and
- liberalisation of capital movements into and out of the country.

Conclusions

Four broad conclusions emerged from the Seminars:
- Privatisation has been slower than expected because of public anger over spontaneous privatisation, uncertainty concerning the contents of prevailing ownership rights, the reluctance of foreigners to invest, and the difficulties inherent in devising an "equitable" privatisation process. There has been much more progress in transferring homes and small businesses from the state sector to the private sector than large firms and land.
- Privatisation alone should not be equated with a substantial improvement in micro efficiency and macro performance. Appropriate incentives, market-oriented institutions and clearly defined property rights should accompany privatisation.
- Policies for macroeconomic stability and efficient allocation of investment include not only elimination of the monetary overhang, anti-inflationary monetary and fiscal policies, and price setting by markets, but also: introduction of new, market-oriented instruments for macroeconomic control; formation of an independent central bank and recapitalised, competitive commercial banks; enterprise restructuring through bankruptcy, privatisation, de-monopolisation, and rehabilitation of viable state enterprises; and creation of regulatory agencies.
- The sequencing debate has produced a consensus that both macro stabilisation measures and institutional reforms are closely related and should be implemented together. Also, each stage in the transformation should embody

as much simultaneity as popular forbearance, budgetary restrictions, skilled labour constraints, and foreign-exchange considerations allow. However, economists remain divided over whether to spend more time searching for an optimal strategy or to act immediately on one of several sensible transformation strategies.

Notes

1. In this paper, pre-perestroika refers to 1988 and earlier. While CPEs can learn a good deal from the privatisation experience of OECD countries, the CPEs' transformation problem involves more than privatisation, namely the creation of markets and market institutions.

2. See, for example, "Die Ungeduld mit dem Wunder", *Frankfurter Allgemeine Zeitung*, 4 August 1990, or "The Ultimate State Bankruptcy Hearing", *Financial Times*, 26 September 1990, on the problems of eastern Germany; "The Birth Pangs of a New Economy", *Financial Times*, 1 August 1990, on Polish reforms; "'Chaos' Charge as Soviet Oil Refining Minister Quits". *Financial Times*, 3 October 1990, on the problems of the Soviet Union.

3. See Hinds (1990) for an analysis and overview.

4. It has been argued that changes in competitive conditions and the regulatory framework tend to have larger effects on incentives and efficiency than ownership transfer *per se* (see Yarrow (1990) and Vickers and Yarrow (1988)). This conclusion might be true for the privatisation of state-owned enterprises already operating within a market economy. However, the initial conditions for state-owned enterprises operating in former CPEs are so different that it is highly unlikely that this view is equally true for these economies.

5. See Yarrow (1990) for details.

6. See Luders (1990), Hinds (1990), and Dhanji and Milanovic (1990) for thoughtful discussion of these points.

References

BLOMMESTEIN, H.J. and M. Marrese, eds., (1991), *Transformation of Planned Economies: Property Rights Reform and Macroeconomic Stability,* OECD, Paris.

BRABANT, J.M. van (1991), "Property Rights' Reform, Macroeconomic Performance, and Welfare", in Blommestein and Marrese, eds., pp. 20-42.

BRAINARD, Lawrence J. (1991), "Strategies for Economic Transformation in central and eastern Europe: Role of Financial Market Reform", in Blommestein and Marrese, eds., pp. 93-107.

CRANE, Keith (1991), "Property Rights Reform: Hungarian Country Study", in Blommestein and Marrese, eds., pp. 64-92.

DHANJI, F. and B. Milanovic (1990), "Privatisation in East and Central Europe: Objectives, Constraints, and Models of Divestiture". Background note for the World Bank Conference on Privatisation and Ownership Changes in East and Central Europe, Washington D.C., 13-14 June.

HINDS, M. (1990), "Issues in the Introduction of Market Forces in Eastern European Socialist Economies", World Bank, EMTTF Division, March.

LUDERS, R.J. (1990), "Chile's Massive Divestiture Programme: 1975-1990, Failures and Successes". Background note for World Bank Conference on Privatisation and Ownership Changes in East and Central Europe, 13-14 June.

MCKINNON, R.I. (1990), "Stabilizing the Ruble: The Problem of Internal Currency Convertibility". Paper prepared for the OECD Development Centre, Paris, 9 July.

NUTI, D. Mario (1991), "Privatisation of Socialist Economies: General Issues and the Polish Case", in Blommestein and Marrese, eds., pp. 51-63.

SCHRETTL, Wolfram (1991), "Structural Conditions for a Stable Monetary Régime and Efficient Allocation of Investment: Soviet Country Study", in Blommestein and Marrese, eds., pp. 108-126.

VICKERS, J.S. and G.K. Yarrow (1988), *Privatisation: An Economic Analysis,* MIT Press, Boston.

WOLF, T.A. (1990), "Reform, Inflation and Adjustment in Planned Economies", *Finance and Development,* March.

YARROW, G.K. (1990), "Privatisation: Issues and Problems". Background note for the World Bank Conference on Privatisation and Ownership Changes in East and Central Europe, Washington D.C., 13-14 June.

Property Rights' Reform, Macroeconomic Performance, and Welfare

Jozef M. van Brabant

One of the pillars of the current sentiment for comprehensive economic and other reforms in central and eastern Europe[1] is privatisation. It is usually lumped together with property rights' reform, although the two may be quite distinct. The protracted discussions about ownership as an inalienable component of property rights reform in these economies have revolved around the assignment of property rights to existing assets as well as on ownership of assets created from gross public and private savings (Hinds 1990a). It is useful to keep the two apart in discussing the merits or drawbacks of privatisation.

Property rights reform is an integral component of the transition to a market economy of the former planned economies. Its main purpose, from an economic perspective, would be to improve the efficiency of resource allocation. Section 1 clarifies the relationship of the transition to a market economy, ownership, and property rights, and why property rights reform is a necessary, but insufficient, condition for improving resource allocation. Alternative ownership forms and their implications are examined next. Section 3 is devoted to the multiple meanings of privatisation and their relevance to central and eastern Europe. The advantages and drawbacks of privatisation are next. Section 5 analyses the difficulties specific to privatisation in central and eastern Europe. Alternative forms of privatising assets in central and eastern Europe are the subject of the final section.

Transition to a market economy, ownership, and property rights reform

A market is almost tautologically concerned with resource allocation. It has little to say about the distribution and possible abuses of ownership, regardless of the great emphasis placed on this element by the neo-Austrian school[2]. Regarding inputs, the issues to be addressed can be separated into the allocation of capital, labour, land, and other natural resources. As for outputs, the principal themes can be reduced to domestic and external trade, the distribution of incomes between consumption and accumulation, and the distribution of time between leisure and work[3]. There is currently little dispute about the need to devolve the entire gamut of trading operations to firms that are financially autonomous. Likewise the choice between work and

The author is a staff member of the Department of International Economic and Social Affairs of the United Nations in New York. The views expressed here are his own and do not necessarily reflect the views that may be held by the United Nations Secretariat.

29

leisure should be left to sovereign decision makers, subject to socio-political rules and agreed institutional arrangements.

The paramount outstanding conceptual issue as regards the market concerns the allocation, maintenance, and formation of capital assets. Indeed, socialists have traditionally viewed public ownership of the means of production as the *sine qua non* for avoiding alienation and exploitation of labour, although neither was achieved in practice. In fact, ownership *per se,* as distinct from capital's services, has little to do with enhancing resource allocation. Certainly, some ownership forms can efficiently allocate the service flows of new or existing capital assets at a smaller cost than others. Of course, one of the most crucial questions facing decision makers in central and eastern Europe at this juncture is what to do with publicly owned capital now that the state has decided in principle to withdraw from exercising direct ownership functions. It is a vexing issue with all kinds of colorations (Tardos 1989, Kornai 1990a). The battle cry of the most liberal reformers, with the active support of outside interest groups, has been for the widespread privatisation of state assets by selling them off or giving them away. Some form of outright privatisation may be especially warranted if capital services can be allocated at lesser cost by internalising the co-ordination process than through a formal market process. But it does not necessarily follow that privatisation should be enacted quickly and below fair market value (Murrell 1990).

The strategy of organising capital markets can best be tackled after recognising two facts. One is that neither private nor public ownership of the means of production by itself guarantees the most efficient use of capital resources. For that, a property environment as neutral as possible must be put in place (Szénási 1989, p. 169). By de-linking, at least conceptually, ownership from ownership rights (all property rights minus the alienation of the assets), one could start thinking about the proper technical issues at stake. A second consideration is that the issue of efficient allocation requires the validation of all property forms. The reason is that there will surely be at least one productive endeavour for which one of the possible formats (private, co-operative, corporate, public, and various mixes) will ensure improved resource allocation. That includes the regulation of entry and exit. If that right is not available to whomever is able to accumulate wealth or entitled to bid on the user rights to wealth, it is hard to envisage how the capital allocation process can be organised efficiently.

Property is concerned with assets in one form or another. These may be tangible, such as fixed assets, or intangible, such as the right of access to airwaves. In that sense, property can be looked at from three different angles, namely the allocation of existing assets, ensuring that existing assets are not eroded for private purposes, and the allocation of new capital. The most acute is the first issue because existing assets in central and eastern Europe are mostly in public hands and there is room for improving returns. Especially here, it is useful to distinguish between ownership *per se* and the usufruct of property rights. Although public ownership established clear property rights[4], the state's overwhelming monopoly on property was confounded by state power, much like in feudal times (Kanel 1974, pp. 828-9). Converting them into secure property rights protected by orderly judicial and legislative procedures limits arbitrary decisions by the powerful. These procedures should also include protection against the erosion of capital assets by those who are not the ultimate owners.

The formation of new capital from amortisation as well as from new public and private savings and how best to ensure that these new assets contribute maximally to the economic benefits raise many questions. In post-war central and eastern Europe,

30

savings for capital-formation purposes was not actively promoted outside the narrow state and co-operative sectors. Firms and households were not encouraged to raise their net asset value as central planners financed investment according to their own criteria. Technically, socialisation is neither necessary nor sufficient for proper resource allocation; neither is privatisation under all circumstances. Certainly, state ownership has a poor record in encouraging technological innovation and adequate maintenance of assets, and it inhibits venture capitalism. For that to flourish, individuals must be able to found their own firm and, hence, to assume the full risk of succeeding or failing with their own or borrowed capital.

There are unquestionably instances in which it would be advisable to encourage private ownership, if only because of the high cost of ensuring proper allocation of user rights to state property. Examples include private housing, small retail outlets, or service firms. On the other hand, precepts on income and wealth distribution and access to a certain social dividend may well counsel for rather than against maintaining state property in basic sectors of economic activity. The same prevails in the case of market failure, notably natural monopoly and externality. But that does not necessarily mean that it would be justified to have the state exert its property rights directly through central planning. The core question would be how to maximise the service flow from such assets as measured by some objective function.

Alternative ownership forms and their implications

Social interaction among individuals, corporations, and government agencies are conditioned by two broad sets of constraints (Ickes 1990, Kanel 1974, Moser 1989). One arises from the physical limit of resources. Behaviour in society is also influenced by rules or institutional arrangements that govern the choices of individual actors. By shaping the structure of incentives, such rules have an important bearing on outcomes. The postulates of constitutional economics imply that if the limits to individual behaviour are well defined and the rights are recognised and accepted, social interaction will proceed in an orderly manner (Kanel 1974).

Without a doubt, alternative property rights exert different effects on the allocation of resources (Demsetz 1967, Furubotn and Pejovich 1972). That the owner of property rights should be entitled to the residual benefits of that ownership is also clear. But there is considerable confusion in the literature (see Alchian 1987, Ryan 1987) about what property rights might entail. In what follows, I consider a property right to be a socially enforced right to select uses of scarce goods. Any mutually agreed contractual terms are permissible, though not all are necessarily enforced by government. That is to say, ownership cannot be satisfactorily defined unless the right of property is the right of dealing with things in the most absolute fashion the law allows (Ryan 1987, p. 1029). The crucial element, in Roman law, is the *ius utendi et abutendi*, that is, the right of use and disposal of the owned object. The latter is very important both as an integral component of property rights and one that can be separated from user rights as such.

An efficient property rights system can be established only by fulfilling at least three conditions (Comisso 1989, pp. 214-5). First, property rights must be lodged in the hands of actors with purely economic responsibilities. In a market context, such rights would of necessity be attributes of the behaviour of private individuals. Although some will also emerge in central and eastern Europe, a good part of the

31

public capital stock for years to come will be used by state-owned enterprises (SOEs). Second, property rights must be enforced by a neutral party based on an effective judicial system and modern civil, fiscal, and commercial codes. This should aim not only at issuing a guarantee that the state would normally not nationalise property, but it should also guarantee the stability of the economic framework, hence reassure those willing to expand their property (Kornai 1990b). Above all, administrative institutions and Party organisations must renounce their powers of direct supervision and restrictive regulation. Finally, policy-making authority, including the ability to prescribe what kinds of activities the bearer of property rights can engage in, must be entrusted to institutions that themselves neither exercise property rights nor enforce them. This is normally the role of the legislative branch of government.

There are two key features of property rights reform. It may be obvious that property rights have to be clearly demarcated. In other words, that limits to individual, corporate, or collective behaviour have to be well defined and mutually recognised, possibly through a social consensus on the tradeoffs between private gain and social welfare. This provides the basis upon which the owners benefit from using that property in the most productive manner or personally bear the cost in the form of reduced returns (Walters 1987, p. 36). At the same time, property rights should not be subject to unpredictable changes resulting from government intervention, confiscation, or nationalisation (Goldberg 1974, Kanel 1974).

Property rights are important in explaining the direction and co-ordination of uses of economic resources in a private property system. By setting the objectives of owners and the systems of monitoring managerial performance, they affect allocative efficiency and exert repercussions on the internal efficiency of firms (Vickers and Yarrow 1988, p. 3). Public and private ownership differ in both respects. Changes in property rights materially affect the incentive structures, hence the behaviour, of management. The transfer of ownership, or entitlements to the residual profits from operating assets, from public to private sectors implies a change in the relationship between those responsible for the firm's decisions and the beneficiaries of its profits. Because the structure of incentives is affected, management modifies its behaviour and performance. The allocative efficiency implications of property assignments depend very much upon the competitive and regulatory environment in which a given firm operates, with the latter two typically having substantially larger effects on performance than ownership per se (Yarrow 1990). It should be stressed, though, that ownership, competition (and hence the monitoring system) and regulation are three sets of influences that are intertwined: the efficiency implications of any change in one set will, as a rule, be contingent upon the other two.

For the decentralised co-ordination of economic decisions to work well along established principles of comparative advantage in a society with diffused knowledge, economic agents must have secure, alienable private property rights in productive resources and products. These rights should be tradeable at mutually agreed prices in reliable contractual transactions that can be negotiated at a fairly low cost[5]. Each type of contract implies different costs of supervision, measurement, and negotiation. Also, the form of economic organisation, along with the function of the visible hand, changes whenever a different contractual arrangement is chosen (Cheung 1987, p. 56). The partitionability, separability, and alienability of private property rights enable the organisation of co-operative joint productive activity in highly specialised economic units, such as the complex corporation (Alchian 1987, p. 1031).

Privatisation and its meanings in central and eastern Europe

The notions of privatisation and property rights reform are widely used in the literature but frequently with considerably different meanings. Many observers take property rights reform to mean divesting state assets to entities (other than state and related government agencies) that can take possession of property; where state ownership involves non-physical assets, such as the right to airwaves or port management, privatisation does, of course, entrust the exploitation of this sector to non-state agents with at best some rent accruing to the state. This transfer involves all angles of property rights, including the alienation of assets (destruction, inheritance, sale, leasing, give-away, and others). Neither is necessary, however, for at least two reasons.

First, outright sale need not at all be involved. Examples would be intangible assets such as the awarding of franchises for the running of public facilities (e.g. naval dockyards) or publicly maintained legal monopolies (e.g. broadcasting rights). The same can apply to tangible assets. Privatisation may simply divorce ownership *per se* from the exercise of most ownership rights. It is even possible to envisage privatisation taking place without a change in the ownership of public assets. Some of the literature on privatisation (Swann 1988, p. 3ff.) encompasses the enjoinment of SOEs to maximise profits, to provide goods and services only if the price covers the incurred cost, and to adopt cost-minimising procedures in employment and procurement. In that sense, though ownership does not change, privatisation alters the balance of power between government as owner and private agents as executors so as to give the latter at least an equal influence over the use of the underlying assets. Others appear to include under privatisation elements of commercialising government production of goods and services by charging user fees (Kent 1987b, p. 13). Second, even when asset sales occur, much of the impact of policy may arise from decisions taken about regulation rather than the transfer of ownership. The immediate effect of privatisation is to substitute shareholder for governmental monitoring and control of the SOE's management. The impact thereof depends very much on the degree to which the new shareholders can motivate management to become more responsive to maximising net asset values. It is not necessarily the case that a simple change in title produces this kind of response.

Privatisation, as a result, can be taken to encompass a wide variety of changes in control over tangible and intangible assets, some of which are concerned with alternative approaches to the supply and indeed financing of local and central government services. As such, privatisation can be described as an umbrella term for a variety of policies loosely linked by the way in which they are taken to mean the strengthening of the market at the expense of the state (Vickers and Wright 1988, p. 1). More specifically, I take privatisation to mean the transfer from the public to the private sector of entitlements to residual profits from operating an enterprise, because that seems to be the preoccupation of the reform debates in central and eastern Europe[6]. This step is usually accompanied by changes in regulatory policy affecting, among others, entry, exit, prices, outputs, services supplied, markets served, consolidations, and profitability.

Seen against the backdrop of the prevailing situation in central and eastern Europe, many arguments can be formulated in favour of privatising state assets. Some are based on purely economic considerations. Others derive essentially from meta-economic assessments. There are furthermore questions regarding divestment of state assets, the state's future role in fixed capital formation, and how to protect the value of state assets. There is certainly no unanimity of views on these issues.

The most cogent arguments for privatisation derive from failures of past reforms and two anomalies of socialism. Foremost are two critical non-economic considerations: the overpowering influence of Party politics over economic affairs and the hold of government bureaucracy over a highly monopolised enterprise sphere. The nomenklatura-appointed management may have earned its spurs in Party politics or obtained a legitimation through the bureaucratic process, but rarely did it manage state assets to maximise the SOE's net worth. Small wonder, then, that the focus of privatisation has been to dissociate political and bureaucratic powers from far-reaching controls over resource allocation (Winiecki 1990, p. 65). To break this grip of the bureaucracy and vested Party interests over resources presents a powerful argument for privatisation as an integral component of a broader-based reform movement, even in circumstances where "market failures" exist and pure theory might suggest more nuanced positions (Lipton and Sachs 1990). Only then will a decision to move away from administrative allocation to a scarcity-oriented allocation process be possible. Often, however, this apodictic statement hides rather than clarifies the political background.

Breaking the back of Party and ministerial controls over economic agents is the single most important argument in favour of privatising assets when the process of eroding the grip of the Communist Party over society is getting under way. Once that is accomplished, as is the case in several central and eastern European countries, it is essentially up to the new government and its parliamentary base to ensure that Party and bureaucracy are removed from management. Economic arguments should now receive a fairer, more technical reading.

State-owned assets represent in essence societal savings enforced through socialist precepts, as seen through the eyes of the ruling élites of the erstwhile planned economy. Although political precepts change, prevailing state assets form part of society's wealth. The custodians of society must, therefore, ensure that these resources are utilised as effectively as possible, given the emerging market environment. This raises two broad areas of inquiry. One deals with the allocation process as such. The other revolves around assigning a proper value to the assets to be privatised, almost regardless of the allocative implications.

Second, the turn taken by reform socialism, entrusting assets essentially to the enterprise collective in some variant of worker self-management, has been a great disappointment. The highly monopolised structure of production in these economies led to economic rents that firms themselves captured rather than the state as owner. But it also led all too easily to raising wages to ensure loyalty to management without the latter putting at risk its own assets or entrenched position. Markets cannot function well without competition, thus require some measure of exit and entry motivated by economic incentives. Furthermore, this decentralisation of ownership has left the legal basis of property rights ill defined. Markets can function well only if rents accrue to those having property rights – not necessarily the ultimate owners who may be content with a fixed rate of return.

Finally, to ensure some equilibrium between equity and economic efficiency, the entire gamut of ownership forms should be fully recognised. Governments interested in divesting themselves of direct involvement in SOEs, yet bent on retaining ownership, can explore at least two alternative organisational forms without disturbing ownership structures. One is arranging leases of assets of SOEs to the highest bidder or to a party determined as the most appropriate in given circumstances; another option is the recognition of management contracts (Vuylsteke 1988, 1990). The advantage is that the benefits of ownership are retained in the public sector, but the operations are, in effect, privatised (Ramanadham 1988b, p. 9). This gives government time to decide on denationalisation and, in the meantime, it helps establish the comparative advantage that the SOE has in the public or private sector. Alternatively, the government could make a genuine declaration to the effect that, irrespective of its ownership, it undertakes not to interfere in the commercial decisions of SOEs.

These alternatives to selling public assets to the private sector presuppose that it is possible to devise criteria of managerial behaviour as surrogates of markets that force an SOE to operate as if it were a private firm. Criteria would include, for example, a specification of minimum required rate of return on capital, targets of overall and perhaps of disaggregated net returns, unit costs and productivity, and the obligation to resort to commercial markets for funds. This leads to a paradox (Zeckhauser and Horn 1989, pp. 55-56): although privatisation may seem most appropriate for SOEs operating in competitive markets, these are precisely the firms whose internal efficiency can be most readily improved by reforms in their public monitoring systems without a change in property rights.

The experience with privatisation in market economies and lessons for central and eastern Europe

The wholesale wave of privatisation attempts in market economies[7] suggests two questions: What were the motivations of these efforts and could they be applied to central and eastern Europe? How successful have these privatisations been and could they provide lessons for central and eastern Europe?

Four basic motives can be associated with the case for privatisation in market economies (Heald 1988, Swann 1988): to improve the use of scarce resources, to plug budget deficits and seek budgetary relief, to serve an ideology that associates freedom and liberty with private ownership and to compress the state to the bare essentials, and to break up entrenched trade-union rights and privileges that inhibit efficient resource allocation. This philosophy contrasts markedly with that prevailing in central and eastern Europe, in part because the latter countries are so far removed from being market economies.

Because the basics of a market economy are yet to be put in place, the main motivation for privatisation has been negative, namely to undercut the power of the bureaucracy and to receive compensation for having been denied non-state property rights. Economists are aware of the allocative implications, but these concerns generally receive short shrift. Related motives may be to enhance freedom and hence the democratic process. For that, some critical minimum of property rights' reform may have to be undertaken quickly, for a democracy without a solid market economy is unthinkable[8].

Although the environment for privatisation in market and planned economies differs substantially, some useful lessons could be derived from the former's experience. Regarding results, one must heed the political philosophy on ownership, the role of trade unions in the post-industrial society, and the social contract through which the policy was pursued. From that narrow perspective, privatisation is by definition a success. But in some cases privatisation had explicit economic and wealth intentions. Whether these can be realised depends very much on restrictions imposed by economic structures and the obstacles encountered in implementing privatisation schemes.

The outcome of privatisation depends very much on the prevailing market structures. Public ownership under conditions of monopoly suffers from a lack of product market competition, and hence incurs productive inefficiency, just like a private monopoly[9]. Unlike the latter, a public monopoly as a rule does not face the threat of bankruptcy as government is likely to bail out SOEs in difficulty. A public monopoly is as a rule also eager to sacrifice cost minimisation for political and trade-union reasons. For SOEs operating under conditions of competition, productive efficiency could be attained. But it would not impose the threat of bankruptcy or take-over, and it would not eliminate the inhibiting effect of political interference in enterprise affairs. Note that the threat of bankruptcy is a potent weapon only when the constraint is active, that is, when firms are in trouble (Ickes 1990, pp. 60-61).

A private monopoly, unlike a public monopoly, (although they are characterised by productive inefficiency because of an absence of product competition) will be under threat of take-over which will keep managers on their toes. But the disciplining role of potential take-overs is not strong and tends to decline with the size of the firm. A private monopoly, however, tends to exploit its market power and cause allocative inefficiency. These considerations need to be compared against any moderation in productive inefficiency, which suggests that private ownership under monopoly might not be superior to public ownership under monopoly. These conflicting influences make the relative performance of public vis-à-vis private monopolies an empirical matter. Finally, private ownership and effective competition yield productive efficiency since product market competition is now reinforced by the market for corporate control. Moreover, the firm faces the possibility of bankruptcy and is not inhibited by government interference. Competitive conditions will also lead prices to be aligned with costs, yielding allocative efficiency.

For markets to function properly, the economies of central and eastern Europe must re-create competition. The latter requires, as Nuti (1990, p. 18ff.) underlines, a sufficient number of autonomous and competitive firms, subject to financial discipline and rewards, capable of responding to market incentives, whose managers are chosen not for political merits but for their professional qualities. To attain this, the monopoly power of large specialised firms and their associations must be removed or substantially reduced. This requires not only physically breaking up the monopolies but also, in case of a natural monopoly, implementing an adequate regulatory framework. Above all, it necessitates breaking the link between the centre and economic agents as regards managerial controls, incentives, and budget dependence.

Such demonopolisation can be pursued by different means. One way of ensuring independence of SOEs from central tutelage is privatisation. But there are other avenues. The elimination of the "petty tutelage" exercised by ministerial bureaucracies should not lead to the dissipation of state ownership. In the smaller countries, even after breaking up the presently existing monopolies, there is unlikely to be sufficient competition in the short run. Liberalisation of the trade regime is the only way in which sufficient competitive pressure can gradually be brought to bear on the performance of industrial firms.

Market structures are, then, key ingredients in the decision to privatise. If that decision is made, many practical obstacles lie ahead. Critical questions are how to evaluate the assets, whether a reservation price should be established, how and how quickly privatisation should proceed, and for what purposes the proceeds should be earmarked. Privatisation in most economies has proceeded in an environment with overwhelming private ownership of the means of production, functioning markets for goods and capital, in most cases integrated capital markets, and with individuals having some culture as regards private enterprise and stockholding. None of these features is strong in central and eastern Europe.

Moreover, has privatisation in market economies succeeded in: lowering product prices, increasing allocative efficiency, raising internal enterprise efficiency, or improving service? Even against this more limited canvas of economic discourse, it is difficult to provide a straightforward answer. Assessments can be grouped essentially under two headings. One is concerned with the question of whether ownership itself is a significant factor in economic performance. Another is whether actual privatisation has demonstrated the superiority of private over public enterprise.

Empirical studies about the relative performance of public and private firms have been inconclusive. Although there is some support for the superiority of private enterprise, this depends critically on the degree of competition prevailing in the market, the incentive structures in alternative organisational forms, and the degree of regulatory policies designed to correct market failures, rather than ownership *per se* (Yarrow 1986, p. 333). These studies illustrate that rarely are such divestments conducted simply on the basis of economic motives, say within a broad and bold competitive approach. Results must therefore be assessed against the backdrop of what originally motivated privatisation. Those advocating privatisation have often been guilty of over-simplification. Sensing the strength of their argument for removal of commercial firms from the non-private sector, they have failed to work through the mechanics of the actual transfer. It is easy to advocate the sale of an SOE. It is much more difficult to specify how the sale should be conducted, to whom, for how much, and how best to allocate the proceeds.

Changes in ownership in the absence of competition and an adequate regulatory environment (Helm and Yarrow 1988) do not inevitably improve performance. This issue is frequently overlooked in the confusion between ownership and competition (Heald 1988, pp. 33-35). Changes in ownership, particularly those accompanied by the creation of competitive conditions, are likely to be beneficial.

The experiences and considerations suggest that the success of privatisation depends on first enacting other components of the transition. Although this paper does not leave sufficient room to elaborate on this issue (see Brabant 1990), the discussion on the desirability of privatising state assets in central and eastern Europe in the rest of this paper advocates implicitly a coarse sequencing. First, all state assets have to be re-nationalised to establish clear property rights. Large monopolies should be quickly broken up into meaningful autonomous units. Other assets, especially housing, handicrafts, and small service centres should be privatised rapidly through open bidding procedures because private property in this case is the most effective way of co-ordinating the service flow of these capital assets. If necessary, sufficient loans with realistic interest rates must be made available. Initially, prices are likely to be volatile. A trustee or trustee organisation appointed with the support of parliament, to which responsibility is owed, should be able to organise such auctions. Regarding land, a bold move forward with de facto land reform would seem to commend itself. Finally, all SOEs (except perhaps those producing strategic goods and public utilities) should be turned into joint-stock companies and placed under the supervision of an impartial body that may have to purchase some state liabilities in exchange for these assets. Again, the trustee should supervise such transfers. At the same time, full property rights have to be established to encourage the formation of new capital from private sources. To foster competition the government may even consider enacting financial inducements, for example, by making low-cost loans available from amortisation funds as well as new savings or by creating transparent fiscal benefits.

The next logical step is to enforce competitive behaviour by creating a regulatory environment and an incentive scheme that will improve the principal-agent problem in SOEs. Gradually, such assets should be opened up for competitive bidding for leases or management contracts, with the supervisory authority being charged with max-imising the return on assets and seeing to it that sufficient insurance schemes are put in place to minimise abuses. At the same time, the government should pursue compre-hensive stabilisation, enact fiscal reform, dilute the power of monopolies, and intro-duce market-type pricing, perhaps by first anchoring key input prices to world prices at a realistic exchange rate.

Once the former SOEs are behaving like competitive firms, and the most urgent structural adjustments have been completed, their privatisation through outright sale should get under way at a measured pace, preferably by feeding the budding domestic stock market or opening discretionary bidding to domestic and foreign entrepreneurs.

Difficulties of privatising state assets in central and eastern Europe

Privatisation should improve the allocation of existing capital assets, maintain the value of these assets, and ensure that new capital is formed and utilised as efficiently as possible. Recall that privatisation is neither necessary nor sufficient to enhance the allocation of capital resources. What is required is the recognition of the usefulness of the entire range of property forms, from outright private ownership all the way to communal property. The principle should therefore be accepted that the choice of one form over another follows, *ceteris paribus,* essentially from the least costly co-ordination of the allocation of the service flows emanating from state assets.

I shall limit privatisation to the divestment of state assets to non-state owners of property rights with the goal of improving the allocative efficiency of the existing capital stock, once constitutional and legal guarantees are firmly and unambiguously in place. Given these conditions, a range of issues must be considered in connection with divestment, utilisation of the usufruct of capital assets, and the improved opera-tion of privatised assets.

38

Proper divestment requires that the real worth of capital assets be turned over to society perhaps to offset some of its liabilities (such as the debt or claims to social services). Reformers should avoid a sellout of existing firms, often through the intermediation of self-interested managers, at prices that deviate substantially from the intrinsic market value of the assets being alienated. This is by no means an easy task, given the problems of establishing a market value for assets that have never been, and cannot quickly be, competitively priced because of prevailing distortions. Market evaluation can begin once a certain volume of shares has been distributed. Only then can a proper value be transferred to private ownership. Each aspect gives rise to many questions that essentially focus on the legacies of central planning and the potential incompetence, malevolence, or lack of control over the rapidly transforming societal processes on the part of reformers.

First of all, the key mechanism of capital formation and distribution in central and eastern Europe has been the state budget, even when SOEs possessed administrative autonomy. Because of the absence of capital markets and the pervasive distortion of relative prices, there is simply no easy way to establish market value on the basis of the discounted value of the expected residual returns to capital over the lifetime of the assets. To circumvent this obstacle, the reforming countries have resorted to makeshift rules that in fact allow one social group to appropriate part of its specialised knowledge by transforming it into a property stake. Not all sales at bargain prices have been on account of incompetence or malevolence on the part of those entrusted with privatisation or their advisers. Lack of transparency inherent in these economies, even when negotiators or existing management has the sincere intention of doing it "right," poses a major obstacle. Determining asset values outside a competitive market environment is a hazardous proposition at best. Of course, the problems get sharply compounded by the fact that the principals in the negotiations are rarely sufficiently scrupulous to avoid deliberately undervaluing assets to appropriate the capital gains directly or indirectly.

Second, the absence of an entrepreneurial class in the emerging market economies has several dimensions. Domestic savings are insufficient to purchase outright a sizeable portion of state assets. In some cases, setting up proper financial institutions, such as independent pension funds, insurance schemes, commercial banks, etc. to whom state liabilities are "sold" can assist in the intermediation. But this cannot be a panacea. Neither is making use of the monetary overhang in some reforming countries, especially when it has been acquired through illegal activities. Legitimate savings could be earmarked for the purchase of housing, small plots of land, and small handicraft or service firms. But it remains to be seen whether ordinary savers are interested in such purchases without there being first substantial other reforms, especially stabilisation, revamping of the fiscal system, wholesale trade, and demonopolisation of SOEs.

Whether it would be worthwhile to privatise enterprises piecemeal, with part of the shares being earmarked for workers at preferential prices is something to be carefully weighed. Perhaps auction markets that are as transparent as circumstances permit, preferably after rationalising SOEs so as not to encumber potential buyers, offer a solution. In the absence of widespread experience with this method of divestment, however, careful experimentation with the organisation of markets and the phasing in of privatisation is warranted.

As a flipside to the absence of an entrepreneurial class, savers tend to be risk-averse. Apart from the uncertainty ensuing from fluctuating share prices, central and eastern Europe has been accustomed to pervasive job and income security over the past fifty years. Although people may wholeheartedly espouse the idea of moving to a market economy, bankruptcy with attendant fluctuations in fortunes may be difficult to accept.

Another side of the absence of capitalism is that state assets have been built up essentially by inhibiting individuals from saving voluntarily. These assets are society's and should be distributed with a considerable degree of egalitarianism. How to do this even if shares are given away poses technical problems that may be difficult to surmount in the short run. A wide distribution of assets would avoid future resentment about giveaways to a favoured class, which is a danger in selling SOEs to their managers at fire-sale prices. It would also ensure support for the temporarily painful measures needed to render those assets more productive, by reforming monetary policy, freeing prices, and ending subsidies. Above all, by greatly strengthening the economic power of the electorate, it would support democracy.

Third, should assets be sold to foreigners? There is nothing wrong with this option if society is willing to accept a dilution of its economic sovereignty and the sale can be conducted in a fair manner. In principle, it should not matter who pays the "proper" price. In fact, foreign influx may be marginally favoured, inasmuch as it is likely to bring into the country badly needed technology and managerial and marketing expertise. But the issue of economic sovereignty cannot be forgotten altogether, particularly in countries whose scope for autonomy was so narrowly circumscribed for so long by Soviet-type precepts. The question is probably less whether to sell assets to foreign owners than in what sectors, to what degree, and how will foreign ownership be regulated.

A fourth problem is the absence of local entrepreuneurship. Exit and entry have traditionally in central and eastern Europe been decided by the centre, generally not in response to the venturesomeness, thrift, and acquisitiveness of society. Furthermore, management of SOEs in these economies has on the whole been entrusted according to priorities that have little to do with its ability to raise the firm's net worth. So even if the state were to withdraw quickly from microeconomic decision making, who would take its place? Further, will would-be managers and entrepreneurs successfully manage and protect assets?

Fifth, SOEs in planned economies do not keep transparent accounts and even those have traditionally been kept from public scrutiny for reasons that transcend the confidentiality legitimately attached to "commercial secrets". It should not be overlooked that management in these countries, as a rule, was never called upon to maximise the SOE's net worth and as a rule had no incentive to do so on its own initiative.

Finally, although productive assets in a planned economy are society's, in some countries it has been unclear for quite some time who is the legal owner of these assets. To correct this confusion, it would be desirable to transfer legal title to SOEs to some trustee charged with divestment, subject to parliamentary scrutiny in the emerging democracies.

40

Private exploitation of the usufruct

Several of the above-cited hindrances surface also when ownership as such is separated from the usufruct, which is leased, contracted out, or otherwise placed at the disposal of private entrepreneurs at some positive rent or even when the state simply enjoins SOE management to behave as private entrepreneurs. The key obstacles in divorcing ownership from its usufruct rest firstly in the determination of the rent to be levied. As a first step, to provide some guidance to auctions, the state could start off the contracting arrangement by offering assets at a positive rent that reflects it own expected rate of return and value of assets. To foster the movement toward a market economy, it may be instructive to let markets set the proper leasing fee with the option of owners to transfer their lease to others willing to outbid them. Certainly, some assets will go below fair value, while others will not find a bid at all. But this loss in revenue may well be a worthwhile investment. Perhaps more difficult would be to enact insurance schemes to protect state assets against the lessee's negligence or misfortune, and to encourage entrepreneurs to upgrade these assets. However, the problems of managerial abilities, fostering a competitive environment, and putting in place adequate regulatory mechanisms remain.

Operating privatised assets

It is often assumed that new owners of privatised assets will by definition allocate their services efficiently and begin to maximise net worth. For a number of reasons, this is by no means guaranteed. It assumes that those acquiring state assets will manage them better than their erstwhile state-appointed caretakers. This is a vastly unrealistic assumption as few individuals in central and eastern Europe have had experience in enterprise management. Planners did not encourage the acquisition of a managerial culture and such skills cannot be acquired quickly but must be built up "on the job".

Related is the assumption that individuals are interested in holding part of their wealth in the form of enterprise shares and will in fact decide to exercise their ownership rights through participation in managerial oversight. That is hardly realistic. In the planned economy, households were not at all encouraged to think in terms of market-based criteria. Stockholding is particularly alien to this mentality. Giving each individual a stake, perhaps on an equitable basis, by distributing public assets would certainly help to create such a culture, but it would take time and mistakes are bound to be committed. Not only that, most households in market economies do not hold a part of their wealth in the form of shares and only some own publicly traded bonds. Even if individuals own shares, they rarely exercise the right to "vote" on management. Participation costs may be very high in some cases. But apathy toward monitoring management and "appointed" directors and "satisficing" of share owners by the management play a more substantial role.

Third, most observers assume that the reforming countries will in due course bring about fair competition in privatised markets. There is simply no guarantee that this will emerge. At the start of the reform, these countries are highly monopolised. Having private monopolies replace state monopolies will not necessarily enhance allocative efficiency or increase the net worth of the firm because competitive bidding is by definition precluded. Unless effective competition and regulation are introduced,

41

the privatisation of firms with market power brings about private ownership in precisely the circumstances where it has least to offer. The desire to privatise speedily, to widen share ownership quickly, and to raise short-term revenue should not stand in the way of devising adequate measures of competition and regulation.

The existence of management that holds a monopoly on information, because of widely dispersed shareholders or of a market monopoly, leads to potentially serious principal-agent problems. If monitoring intensity is low, managers have discretion to pursue their own objectives rather than those held by owners. It is therefore important to structure incentives so as to make management behave according to the instructions of owners. It is important to ensure that the firm's monopoly of information is broken and the regulator has independent access to detailed information, for example, on the potential for cost reduction and the relative costs of services supplied by a multi-product firm[10].

Fourth, two hundred years of experience with capitalism has made it clear that there are numerous imperfections in the market mechanism. At the same time, experiments with other allocation arrangements suggest that there is no alternative to a market mechanism if the economy is to progress steadily. To avoid the worst negative side effects, yet enhance the positive features of the market mechanism, a well-entrenched and adequate regulatory mechanism in the hands of an impartial body is absolutely necessary. Only then can private interests be harmonised with society's.

Finally, thriving competition must apply also to the acquisition and disposal of private assets. For that, it is necessary to have in place adequate capital markets, including safeguards and regulatory mechanisms against abuses. A proper capital market can function only if the regulatory mechanisms are in place and there is sufficient transparency in the market. For that, firms must adhere to certain supervisory and accounting rules that foster competition among economic agents on the basis of expected returns to capital.

Alternative forms of privatisation

Privatisation can take many different forms. I shall consider here spontaneous privatisation (essentially giving away assets to enterprises, workers, or society at large); selling assets through some divestment mechanism; and seeking to divorce ownership from the usufruct of assets.

Spontaneous privatisation means that those entrusted with state assets take possession of them, then turn them into a joint company, part of which can be transferred to clear owners. Hungary initially chose this route because decision makers wished to avoid re-nationalisation of assets. The experience has not been a promising one (Lee and Nellis 1990). Financially, spontaneous privatisation allows individuals to become owners without paying a fair price and thus deprives the government of needed revenues to offset its liabilities. Economically, there is no reason to believe that resource allocation will improve by turning over assets to people who formerly ran these facilities poorly. Being entrusted with assets, management may change its allegiance and in view of the incentives behave significantly differently than they did as state employees. But there is no guarantee that they will potentially do better than other asset holders. Furthermore, free distribution may exacerbate already existing inflationary pressures on account of wealth effects (Nuti 1990, p. 20). Politically, management in place has frequently been appointed under the nomenklatura rules. At the very least, conflict of interest laws should have been used to prevent managers from laundering state assets through dummy corporations that they created in the private sector (Lipton and Sachs 1990). There is also bound to be an equity problem. Worker ownership might be fine for those employed in profitable operations, but not for those in persistent loss-making ventures. Of course, those not employed in SOEs who nonetheless involuntarily contributed to asset formation would be excluded altogether. Finally, there is an organisational problem with worker management in the sense that those belonging to the former managerial group, who have the experience and know-how to supervise the firms, may be eliminated from the new team.

The fact that state assets were publicly formed and treated as society's is the argument used to justify simply distributing these assets free of charge, regardless of wealth effects (Hinds 1990a). The most common form recommended has been worker management of SOEs, essentially an extension of the labour-managed firm. This encourages the maximisation of income per worker rather than the long-run profit of the firm, particularly when there is no capital market where workers can voluntarily sell their right to participate in future profit earnings at a market valuation based on the expected earnings of the enterprises. That is to say, worker management is insufficient to ensure efficiency; ownership and a market for trading such property are also required.

The second form is distributing property to workers on the ground that ownership in state firms should be transferred to the existing workers, who will then be requested to improve the firm's profitability. The key assumption of such transfer is that property owners would automatically improve the allocation process and thereby render the firm profitable. Such an assumption is fallacious. It is also an inequitable solution. The value of capital per worker in state firms varies a great deal for reasons that have nothing to do with the relative merits of the present labour force. Also, free distribution of assets fails to provide government revenue. Furthermore, it tends to favour reinvestment in existing types of activities under present management and to continue employment of the present labour force.

Whereas the labour-managed firms suffer from weak principles, some employee share-ownership program (ESOP) is worth considering, especially if it could be coupled with promises to limit demands for monetary compensation, to foster productivity, to change work rules, and other measures that give workers a material stake in their firm. But this could be accomplished without outright privatisation by creating a joint-stock company, whose performance incentives include obtaining a share in the firm's capitalised value.

Third, property can also be distributed to society at large. There are good reasons to do so as state assets have been accumulated through confiscation or forced savings. To ensure some measure of equity in the distribution of assets, rather than grant ownership rights to the labour force of existing SOEs, they could be distributed to the population at large, either on an individual basis or by households. This form of divestment is also advocated in view of the inadequacies of capital markets and the shortage of domestic capital in reforming countries (Hinds 1990b). Although intuitively appealing, this form has serious drawbacks, apart from the wealth effects at a time of already significant inflationary pressures. There are bound to be potential losers, including those holding the debt of these governments (Vanous 1989, p. 6). It would also erode the corporate taxation base particularly in the absence of a personal income tax. Moreover, privatisation deprives the government of the future stream of revenues from assets and should ideally be accompanied by the retirement of state obligations. Privatisation without revenue raising does not offer this possibility and makes the need for fiscal reform of personal income taxation more urgent. Furthermore, if shares are distributed equitably, any one household would hold only a minuscule interest in any of the enterprises. The distinction between the pre- and a post-reform situation would be largely nominal. Greater concentration of ownership might come through the creation of several mutual funds, and their random allocation to households (Feige 1990). But how to ensure that each household receives portfolios of approximately equal value, given serious asset-valuation problems in these countries, is a conundrum that needs to be resolved. Unquestionably the most serious shortcoming of this path to privatisation is that no beneficial effect is exerted on management and the allocation of resources. The population at large is unlikely soon to become sophisticated investors or attend board meetings. Even mutual fund managers will not have the knowledge or incentive to assess managerial performances and promote take-overs when needed, hence the serious monitoring problems that are embedded.

Another alternative to the previous forms of privatisation is to divorce ownership from the usufruct of assets. Custodial rights over the use of social property could be traded in functioning capital markets. If so, can it lead to a more effective allocation of scarce resources than attained with traditional management of SOEs? An answer can usefully be formulated by first looking at the stationary state and then at one where there is positive growth of the capital stock. With a stationary state, central policy makers must impose proper charges and safeguards to ensure that capital users do not erode assets. In principle, it is entirely feasible to let economic agents bid on the right to use society's capital, to set up a mandatory insurance scheme to protect the capital stock, and to let firms fail when unable to pay the net charge for the usufruct.

In a growing economy, questions of how additions to the capital stock and its replacement are decided upon loom large. These problems include how best to facilitate exit and entry as well as how to ensure that the capital stock will be steadily upgraded. Both additions to and replacements of the existing capital stock could be handled through exit and entry by entrepreneurs bidding on access to future assets. This could be organised through full-fledged capital markets, including those for forward transactions. Entrepreneurs, with the assistance of financial institutions, would simply explore how best to allocate society's savings, including amortization funds and state savings.

Given the complexity of ensuring the efficient functioning of all these markets even in mature market economies, however, it is hard to see how the emerging market economy could create such refined capital markets within a comparatively brief period of time at a tolerable transaction cost. In fact, multiple ownership forms in combination with the gradual emergence of capital markets for the bulk of society's capital may well be the more desirable way of proceeding because they internalise coordination at a smaller cost than through full-fledged capital markets. Such dilution of property rights would be based on economic grounds rather than on the ideology of wealth distribution.

Finally, privatisation may involve the outright sale of assets through auctions or more discretionary channels. Of course, questions concerning how to establish prices and what to do with the proceeds remain. Apart from the fact that auction markets would have to be organised, the sale of state assets calls into question the availability of funds, whether households prefer to hold wealth in company shares, and the desirability of setting a reservation price. To mitigate the lack of funds and to entice individuals into adopting a share-holding culture, one of the more appealing forms of selling off state assets is through debt-financed auctions. This would make available generous financial resources to those willing to acquire state assets and able to manage them profitably. In essence, the state as lender would become a rentier while private sectors end up capitalist debtors (Lipton and Sachs 1990, p. 76).

Whereas it would in principle be possible to conduct auctions with a clear reservation price, the ambience in which this would have to be carried out probably rules out the imposition of a realistic reservation price. That could be implemented much more safely through a discretionary divestment program. Determining a reasonable reservation price and ensuring that the discretionary sale would not infringe upon society's rights or extend favours that one was trying to rule out are no simple tasks. Regarding the determination of a reservation price, some carefully conducted research by custodians of property under the supervision of the newly formed parliamentary organs, perhaps with the assistance of outside accounting firms, should yield a plausible range of asset values. For most undertakings, there should be some positive price that can be realistically established with some good will on the part of all actors involved. The latter should be denied the right to acquire ownership rights to reduce the room for conflicts of interest.

Conclusions

The preceding analysis has hopefully injected an element of scepticism into the desirability of fast and widespread privatisation in central and eastern Europe. While a number of benefits have been claimed for privatisation, "many of its goals are better achieved by other policies and... it is on its contributions to economic efficiency that privatisation must ultimately be judged" (Yarrow 1986, p. 324). In the case of emerging market economies, scepticism is warranted for all the reasons cited for mature market economies plus at least two others. One is that there are ways other than privatisation to break up the massive hold of Party and bureaucracy over economic affairs. Breaking that hold is strategic to putting in place the critical minimum impulse to the development of genuine markets. The other derives from the highly monopolised industrial structure of central and eastern Europe.

My analysis suggests therefore that quickly undertaking a massive program of ill-prepared privatisation for ideological, political, or sentimental reasons may lead to "*une économie de casino*" (Vickers and Wright 1988, p. 25). This is an unjustified way for the state to divest itself of society's assets, no matter how badly these resources may be utilised now. Under no circumstance could privatisation be considered a panacea for raising economic efficiency. That depends critically on the creation of a competitive environment and the recognition in principle of the validity of all alternative property rights.

Notes

1. Central and eastern Europe here comprises Bulgaria, Czechoslovakia, the former German Democratic Republic, Hungary, Poland, and Romania. Much of what is said here about property rights and privatisation would apply also to the Soviet Union. But since the latter has not yet unambiguously decided for a transition to a market economy and privatisation, I focus here chiefly on the general situation of the most reform-minded countries of Eastern Europe.

2. The argument of that school (see Leipold 1983, 1988; Pejovich 1987, 1989, 1990) depends critically on the existence of freedom of entry at the pre-production stages of the competitive process (Yarrow 1986, p. 345). If barriers to entry into production are high, entry is also deterred at an early stage. Also, pure individualism and that it can avoid social conflicts are key, but unrealistic assumptions.

3. Whether "output" on the resource ledger can be negative or should be held nominally constant is a matter that society must decide upon, otherwise the notorious short-range outlook of markets leads to market failure.

4. In some cases, however, efforts made in the mid-1980s to improve economic performance through administrative devolution resulted in ill-defined property rights. Enterprises disposed of the capital stock but it was not at all clear whether they were the owners in full control of assets.

5. If transaction costs are zero, given Coase's theorem, alternative institutional or organisational arrangements would provide no basis for choice and hence could not be interpreted by economic theory.

6. For other forms of privatisation, see Vicker and Wright 1988, p. 3.

7. For useful details, see Bauer 1988; Bianchi, Cassese, and Sala 1988; Buckland 1987; Drumaux 1988; Heald 1988; Kent 1987a; MacAvoy, Stanbury, Yarrow, and Zeckhauser 1989; Nankani 1988, 1990; Ramanadham 1988a; Swann 1988; Vickers and Wright 1988; Vickers and Yarrow 1988; Yarrow 1986.

8. Recall that there continues to be considerable egalitarian thinking in these countries and a strong public sentiment for economic equality in spite of the fact that economic differentiation is bound to occur through the transition to a market economy, even if at the start of privatisation equality of share holding can be ensured.

9. But public ownership need not imply state monopoly just like private ownership need not forcibly foster competition (Vickers and Yarrow 1988, p. 45).

10. Widespread ownership inevitably dilutes the monitoring role of owners and hence modifies the behaviour of management so that it no longer maximises the net worth of the firm's assets. This point is often ignored in the zealous advocacy of privatisation (see Feige 1990, Leipold 1988, Pejovich 1990, Schroeder 1988).

46

References

ALCHIAN, Armen A. (1987), "Property rights", *The New Palgrave – A Dictionary of Economics,* Vol. 3, Macmillan, London, pp. 1031-34.

BAUER, Michel (1988), "The Politics of State-Directed Privatisation: The case of France, 1986-88," *West European Politics,* 4, pp. 49-60.

BIANCHI, Patrizio, Sabino Cassesse and Vincent della Sala (1988), "Privatisation in Italy: aims and constraints", *West European Politics,* 4, pp. 87-100.

BRABANT, Jozef M. van (1990), *Remaking Eastern Europe – on the Political Economy of Transition,* Kluwer, Dordrecht, (forthcoming).

BUCKLAND, Roger (1987), "The costs and returns of the privatization of nationalized industries", *Public Administration,* 3, pp. 241-57.

CHEUNG, Steven N.S. (1987), "Economic organization and transaction costs", *The New Palgrave – A Dictionary of Economics,* Vol. 2, Macmillan, London, pp. 55-57.

COMISSO, Ellen (1989), "Property rights in focus," *Acta Oeconomica,* 4, pp. 210-16.

DEMSETZ, Harold (1967), "Toward a theory of property rights," *The American Economic Review,* Papers and Proceedings, 2, pp. 347-59.

DRUMAUX, Anne (1988), "Privatisation in Belgium: the national and international context", *West European Politics,* 4, pp. 74-86.

FEIGE, Edgar L. (1990), "Perestroika and Socialist Privatisation: what is to be done: and how?", University of Wisconsin, Madison, January, (mimeo).

FURUBOTN, Eirik G.and Svetozar Pejovich (1972), "Property rights and economic theory: a survey of recent literature", *The Journal of Economic Literature,* 2, pp. 1137-62.

GOLDBERG, Victor P. (1974), "Public choice – property rights," *Journal of Economic Issues,* 3, pp. 555-79.

HEALD, David (1988), "The United Kingdom: privatisation and its political context", *West European Politics,* 4, pp. 31-48.

HELM, Dieter and George Yarrow (1988), "The assessment: the regulation of utilities", *Oxford Review of Economic Policy,* 2, pp. i-xxxi.

HINDS, Manuel (1990a), "Issues in the introduction of market forces in Eastern European socialist economies", The World Bank, Washington D.C., March, (mimeo).

HINDS, Manuel (1990b), "Issues in the introduction of market forces in Eastern European socialist economies", Annex I "Enterprise reform issues", The World Bank, Washington D.C., March, (mimeo).

ICKES, Barry W. (1990), "Obstacles to economic reform of socialism: an institutional-choice approach", *Annals of the American Academy of Political and Social Sciences,* 1, pp. 53-64.

KANEL, Don (1974), "Property and economic power as issues in institutional economics," *Journal of Economic Issues,* 4, pp. 827-40.

KENT, Calvin A., ed., (1987a) *Entrepreneurship and the privatizing of government,* Quorum Books, New York-Westport, CO.

KENT, Calvin A., (1987b) "Privatization of public functions: promises and problems", in Kent (1987a), pp. 3-22.

KING, Timothy (1990), "Foreign direct investment in the East European economic transition", The World Bank, Washington, D.C., March, (mimeo).

KORNAI, János, (1990a) *The road to a free economy – shifting from a socialist system: the example of Hungary,* W.W. Norton & Company, New York.

KORNAI, János, (1990b) *The affinity between ownership and coordination mechanisms – the common experience of reform in socialist countries,* World Institute for Development Economics Research, Helsinki.

LEE, Barbara and John Nellis (1990), "Enterprise reform and privatization in market economies", The World Bank, Washington, D.C., April (mimeo).

LEIPOLD, Helmut, (1983) "Eigentumsrechte, Öffentlichkeitsgrad und Innovationsschwäche – Lehren aus dem Systemvergleich", in *Innovationsproblemein Ost und West,* eds. Alfred Schüller, Helmut Leipold, and Hannelore Hamel, Gustav Fischer Verlag, Stuttgart, pp. 51-64.

LEIPOLD, Helmut, (1988) *Wirtschafts und Gesellschaftssysteme im Vergleich,* 5th edn., Gustav Fischer Verlag, Stuttgart.

LIPTON, David and Jeffrey Sachs (1990), "Creating a market economy in Eastern Europe: the case of Poland". Paper prepared for the Brookings Panel on Economic Activity, 5-6 April.

MacAVOY, Paul W., W.T. Stanbury, George Yarrow, and Richard J. Zeckhauser, eds., (1989) *Privatization and state-owned enterprises – lessons from the United States, Great Britain and Canada,* Kluwer, Boston-Dordrecht-London.

MOSER, Peter (1989), "Toward an open world order: a constitutional economics approach", *The Cato Journal,* 1, pp. 133-47.

MURRELL, Peter (1990), "'Big Bang' versus evolution: East European economic reforms in the light of recent economic history", *PlanEcon Report,* 26.

NANKANI, Helen B., (1988) *Techniques of privatization of state-owned enterprises – volume II: selected country case studies,* The World Bank, Washington, D.C.

NANKANI, Helen B. (1990), "Lessons of privatization in developing countries," *Finance & Development,* 2, pp. 43-45.

NUTI, Domenico Mario (1990), Stabilization and sequencing in the reform of socialist economies, The World Bank, Washington, D.C. Paper prepared for the seminar on "Managing inflation in socialist economies," Laxenburg, 6-8 March.

PEJOVICH, Svetozar (1987), "Freedom, property rights and innovation in socialism," *Kyklos,* 4, pp. 461-75.

PEJOVICH, Svetozar (1989), "Liberty, property rights, and innovation in Eastern Europe", *The Cato Journal,* 1, pp. 57-71.

PEJOVICH, Svetozar (1990), "A property-rights analysis of the Yugoslav miracle", *Annals of the American Academy of Political and Social Sciences,* 1, pp. 123-32.

RAMANADHAM, V.V., ed., (1988a) *Privatisation in the UK,* Routledge, London-New York.

RAMANADHAM, V.V., (1988b) "The concept and rationale of privatisation", in *Privatisation in the UK,* ed. V.V. Ramanadham, Routledge, London-New York, pp. 3-25.

RYAN, Alan, (1987) "Property", *The new Palgrave – a Dictionary of Economics,* Vol.3, Macmillan, London, pp. 1029-31.

48

SCHROEDER, Gertrude E. (1988), "Property rights issues in economic reforms in socialist countries," *Studies in Comparative Communism*, 2, pp. 175-88.

SWANN, Dennis, (1988) *The retreat of the state – deregulation and privatization in the UK and US*, The University of Michigan Press, Ann Arbor, MI.

SZÉNÁSI, M. (1989), "A dispute on the changes in property rights", *Acta Oeconomica*, ½, pp. 165-72.

TARDOS, Márton (1989), "Economic organizations and ownership", *Acta Oeconomica*, ½, pp. 17-37.

VANOUS, Jan (1989), "Privatization in Eastern Europe: possibilities, problems, and the role of western capital", *PlanEcon Report*, 38/39.

VICKERS, John and Vincent Wright (1988), "The politics of industrial privatisation in Western Europe: an Overview", *West European Politics*, 4, pp. 1-30.

VICKERS, John and George Yarrow, (1988) *Privatization: an economic analysis*, The MIT Press, Cambridge MA.

VUYLSTEKE, Charles, (1988) *Techniques of privatization of state-owned enterprises*, Vol.I "Methods and implementation", The World Bank, Washington, D.C.

VUYLSTEKE, Charles (1990), "Privatization in emerging economies – constraints and practical responses". Paper prepared for the conference on "Privatization and Ownership Changes in East and Central Europe" World Bank, Washington, D.C., 13-14 June.

WALTERS, Alan Rufus, (1987) "Privatization: a viable policy option?", in Kent, (1987a) pp. 35-64.

WINIECKI, Jan (1990), "Obstacles to economic reform of socialism: a property-rights approach," *Annals of the American Academy of Polical and Social Sciences*, 1, pp. 65-71.

YARROW, George, (1986) "Privatization in theory and practice," *Economic Policy, No. 2*, pp. 324-77.

YARROW, George (1990), "Privatization: issues and problems". Paper prepared for the conference on "Privatization and Ownership Changes in East and Central Europe", World Bank, Washington, DC, 13-14 June.

ZECKHAUSER, Richard J. and Murray Horn, (1989) "The control and performance of state-owned enterprises," in MacAvoy, Stanbury, Yarrow, and Zeckhauser, pp. 7-57.

Privatisation of Socialist Economies: General Issues and the Polish Case

Mario Nuti

Summary

The current drive towards privatisation by transitional economies of central and eastern Europe is based on the same expectation as privatisation in Western countries, i.e. greater efficiency through changed and improved incentives. This expectation is not controversial in the centrally planned economies in transition, because it is believed that privatisation will inject life into the inert traditional system, de-politicise economic life and harden budget constraints. In addition, private property was never completely abolished and a limited régime of private property seems to be inherently unstable, given the strong logical arguments and actual pressures for its extension.

There are three main general issues raised by privatisation of the transitional economies of central and eastern Europe. First, in the early stages of economic reform and in order to free enterprise there is the danger of divesting central organs of their powers without transferring those powers to other agents. This raises on the one hand the problem of "re-subjectivisation" of ownership before privatisation, and on the other the problem of workers' self-management institutions. Next, there is the risk of unfair private appropriation – whether legal or "wild" – of state assets. Last, when should privatisation occur in the sequence of reform measures relative to stabilisation, demonopolisation, and partial financial and productive restructuring?

In Poland, privatisation has been facilitated by a long-standing tradition of private enterprise, but rendered difficult by the necessity to reconcile the sale of shares with the self-management institutions active in Polish enterprises (to be accomplished perhaps by reserving 20 per cent or so of shares to enterprise employees on privileged terms, or by a contractual package involving forms of profit sharing and "Mitbestimmung"). The debate in Poland has revolved primarily around the adverse distributional impact of privatisation, which sectors to begin with, the small size of the potential market, how to finance share purchases (free shares, credit or foreign capital), and the scope for debt-equity swaps. These issues reflect political struggle:

An earlier version of this paper was presented at the OECD Conference on "The Transformation of Planned Economies", Paris, on 20th-22nd June 1990. Acknowledgements for useful comments and suggestions are due to *Grzegorz Kolodko* and to Conference participants, in particular to *William Evers* as discussant, and to the Proceedings editors *Hans Blommestein* and *Michael Marrese.* Responsibility for opinions, errors and omissions rests solely with the author.

the 15th version of the privatisation law was presented to Parliament in April 1990, and was met by a parliamentary counter-proposal. Although the law was finally approved in July 1990, it left open both the pace and modality of privatisation, further delaying progress towards privatisation.

Introduction

Today all the socialist economies of central and eastern Europe are restoring or expanding forms of private ownership and enterprise. The process involves all these "transitional" economies, regardless of the pace and achievements of their economic reform, including the Soviet Union and excluding only Albania; differences are only of speed, mode and degree. There is privatisation in a broad sense (the permission and encouragement of private enterprise and ownership), and in the narrow sense (the sale, gift or rental of state assets to private individuals and companies). This paper considers the general case for privatisation in the narrow sense (Section 2) and in the light of the system-specific characteristics of socialist economies (Section 3); additional reasons are offered for the resilience of private ownership in socialist economies and the mounting pressure for its extension (Sections 4-6). Some more general issues are considered in the current process of privatisation in the transitional economies of central and eastern Europe (Sections 7-9), with a more specific focus on the privatisation process in Poland (Sections 10-12).

The general case for privatisation

To a great extent the drive towards privatisation in central and eastern Europe has the same basis as a similar process also seen in the last ten years in Europe, North America, Japan and the Third World (see Hemming and Mansoor 1988; Vickers and Yarrow 1988). The strongest reason for this development is the expectation that privatisation can raise efficiency through changed incentives.

This expectation is found in the recent economic literature on principal-agent relations. Company managers, as agents of owners, are subject to contractual discipline enforced by shareholders; to take-over discipline enforced by potential bidders; and to bankruptcy discipline enforced by creditors. Managers of state enterprises are not subject to any such discipline, as they are subordinated to political authority and not to economically motivated shareholders; they are not subject to take-overs; and their losses are absorbed by automatic grants from the state budget (see Vickers and Yarrow 1988). Further arguments for privatisation have been the adoption of a deflationary fiscal stance less austere than it would be if implemented through fiscal means, and the promotion of diffused ownership patterns associated with the "property-owning democracy" model as an alternative to socialism.

These arguments for privatisation may have to be modified. Public enterprises sometimes can be more efficient than their private counterparts (in practice, see South Korean state steel; in theory, see Sappington and Stiglitz 1987, Stiglitz 1989). Privatisation of management might achieve the same effects as privatisation of ownership without divesting the state of its assets (i.e. the state could hold shares in private companies; see Meade 1989). In Western market economies, privatisation has not

52

been accompanied by significant progress towards property-owning democracy. In the case of transitional economies, however, privatisation not only raises the share of national assets held by private owners, it also extends the scope of ownership rights from absent or limited ownership to full-fledged private ownership. This qualitative aspect of privatisation in transitional economies provides additional system-specific, supportive arguments.

System-specific arguments for privatisation in socialist economies

First, there is a presumption that privatisation will inject life into the inert traditional system. With the benefit of hindsight the main drawback of central planning and state ownership has been its inability to respond to change (whether in technology, domestic demand, or world trade opportunities); the appropriation of the benefits that economic agents might obtain from faster response can only enhance the vitality and viability of those economies.

Second, privatisation is bound to weaken the opportunity for political interference in economic life, especially in those economies still dominated by the Communist Party and its all-pervasive "nomenklatura". In principle it should be possible to cut the links between the centre and enterprises by inserting an intermediate layer of independent state holdings representing state interests. In this context privatisation may not be necessary, but it is an effective, well-tested institution and therefore more appealing than more controversial and less well-tried state holdings.

Third, privatisation of enterprises and commercial banks together is bound to harden the "soft" budget constraint of enterprises, which has been one of the main sources of the endemic excess demand typical of centrally planned economies everywhere. Again, it is conceivable that the budget of a state enterprise might be hardened as a result of a change in government policy, but in the light of experience there is little – if any – support for this expectation.

Whatever the validity and strength of the general justification, these three arguments strengthen the case for the privatisation now occurring in transitional economies. But there is more: privatisation appears also as the consequence of the resilience of private ownership in socialist economies, and there is a strong case for the further extension of the limited property rights which already have existed.

The resilience of private ownership

Private ownership seems to have a built-in resilience in the socialist economies, where it was never completely eradicated. Moreover, regimes of limited ownership seem to suffer from a certain institutional instability: whenever private ownership is even minimally present, the system tends naturally towards its further extension.

Let us consider what is the necessary and sufficient condition for complete abolition of private ownership. Imagine an economy where individuals have access to instant consumption of goods and services, whether freely (in unlimited amounts or within predetermined limits for each good and service) or subject to money prices and a maximum money budget per unit of time. In either case we stipulate that in this economy individuals do not have any other access to consumption and are not able to transfer their consumption claims to others or over time, i.e. they cannot save in the sense of accumulating that part of their maximum consumption entitlement which they do not actually consume. This is the kind of partial or temporary arrangement familiar from expense accounts, communal kibbutz consumption or participation in academic conferences but – with the possible though unproven exception of Stone Age economies – such an arrangement has never been a basis for the lasting economic organisation of entire communities. Free unlimited consumption, the ultimate full communist model[1], belongs to this category but has never been implemented anywhere; "realised socialism" has never organised consumption on that basis.

The lack of a generalised system of consumption allocation of this kind is a necessary and sufficient condition for private property to arise. Namely, it is a necessary condition because otherwise property could not be transferred, rented or used without violating our stipulations. It is a sufficient condition because a possible private property right on consumption goods arises as soon as claims to consumption can be transferred to others (creating the possibility of future reciprocity, whether through market exchange or possibly through a deferred exchange of reciprocal gifts) or to oneself over time through production or through storage of either the goods or the claims.

It is interesting to note that money is a sufficient but not a necessary condition for private ownership to arise: even in a system without either money or voucher claims and with short-lived goods only (the least favourable set up for property rights to consumption to arise), a stock of consumption goods can be carried and owned within the constraints set by the rate of durability and by the storage space available, the actual stock being determined possibly as the result of an optimisation process leading to the equalisation of rates of time preference and expected rates of return on each consumption good accumulated[2]. Once there is money – at least in the limited role of a means of distributing consumption goods – and this money is non-perishable[3], the possibilities of amassing potential command over a stock of consumption goods become virtually unlimited even if all goods were perishable and no storage space were available. The actual stock of money held will be limited, though, by the same optimisation process, whereby the real rate of time preference is set equal to the real rate of return on money holdings, i.e. the percentage cost of money storage[4] minus the expected rate of money price increase, for all goods.

This reasoning presumes that "markets" clear, though it does not necessarily imply a supply schedule, only that given quantities of dated consumption goods are available and distributed at state-fixed prices. Market clearing is an inappropriate assumption for traditional socialist economies, which are inordinately prone to permanent excess demand due to the unreasonable overambition of planned targets, combined with an unsustainable commitment to stable prices. However, a claim to a stock of consumption goods can be held in real terms and (through money) even in conditions of persistent shortages except that the relevant prices are official money prices plus a premium for queuing or for random access to goods. Secondary retrading of shortage goods, whether it exists legally or illegally, will necessarily tend toward this relevant price level.

It follows from these reflections on theoretical consumption behaviour that, when we discuss private property under models of socialism other than the (unrealised) full communist model, we cannot bring into question the possibility of private property, which is always there at least in the form of some property rights to a stock of consumption goods, nor the existence of a rate of return (negative though it may be in real terms) on that stock. We can only discuss the scope of those property rights and the way that rate of return is determined. Namely, we can discuss who can own what for what purpose, the unbundling of property into its constituent rights (as simultaneous *jus utendi, fruendi ac abutendi* in Roman law, with possible finer distinctions in modern times), their yield and their transferability to whom, and how the efficiency implications of private property respond to progressively increasing extensions of the scope of private property. We can also discuss the set of possible limitations or obligations which may be attached to property rights. Finally, we can discuss whether and to what extent the effects of private property might be simulated by alternative arrangements.

The case for extension of limited property rights

The presence of property rights to consumption goods is an apparently harmless consequence, of permitting individual choice of how to allocate consumption over time, an arrangement which is both efficient and – arguably – a basic freedom. However, once this limited scope of property rights is established there are very strong logical arguments on efficiency grounds, and in response to actual economic pressures, for their extension to a full-fledged capitalist regime of property rights – where anybody can own and trade anything except drugs and slaves, and rights can be unbundled and transferred at will[5].

In fact, if I am allowed to save real consumption and retain its ownership at a real rate of interest implicit in storage conditions, obviously I should be given the opportunity to save instead in the form of cash and interest-yielding deposits and bonds at a nominal monetary rate of interest equivalent to the same real rate, thus releasing real resources for productive use. Indeed, if I am willing to save more and more at progressively higher interest rates, and there are correspondingly profitable productive uses for those resources, I should be given that opportunity for the sake of efficiency. This multiplies the possibility of accumulating private property by relaxing storage and perishability constraints and of receiving a rentier income.

Any investment in consumption goods has an element – albeit small – of risk-taking, depending on current conditions (should I invest in an umbrella or in sunglasses?) affecting the course of relative prices. Financial claims broaden the scope of potential exposure to risk and to its rewards or penalties; loans can be at fixed or variable interest rates; borrowers' creditworthiness will be reflected in their cost of finance. Even in the absence of risk-taking in financial markets, lotteries may and usually do exist in any socialist economy[6]. Moreover employment contracts even under socialism often carry performance-related bonuses, uncertain and lottery-like, broadening further the scope of risk-taking. But now, if I am allowed to draw an interest on financial claims and to expose myself to risk for the sake of a higher expected return, why should I be barred from owning a stake in the present value of an "enterprise" (defined broadly as a set of productive activities and contractual rights and obligations). In a world where there are interest rates and risk premia the introduction of private shares and capital markets does not involve a qualitative change. At first shares may be issued to workers of the same enterprise and may not carry a vote; risk-spreading however suggests a reshuffling of stock across enterprises through generalised trade in a stock exchange, and managerial discipline requires the subjection of managers to the threat of an adverse majority vote (and the take-over threat of vote-acquiring bidders).

Finally, once I am allowed to hold an equity stake in an enterprise, and share in its success and failure, there is no qualitative change involved in my being allowed to directly found and run an enterprise and employ workers directly rather than through the mediation of managers[7]. Down the slippery slope of property rights, through small Pareto-improving steps, one may quickly revert to full-fledged traditional capitalism.

Over time, the case for privatisation mounts implacably with the accumulation of successive monetary gaps between income and expenditure, due to the excess demand systematically present in the socialist economy and the stubborn commitment to maintain stable prices in spite of it. The overhang takes the form of excess liquid assets and abnormally high levels of stocks, both by households and enterprises[8]. In the end the domestic overhang becomes so large as to suggest the selling of state assets to the population instead of alternatives which may be more unpalatable (currency confiscation, hyperinflation) or simply not available (additional domestic or international borrowing).

Ownership and entrepreneurship

An interesting question is whether there is a natural breaking point in this chain, i.e. where – if anywhere – do decreasing returns set in on the road to full capitalist ownership. According to Mises, private ownership of capital is a necessary precondition of capital markets and therefore of markets in general; without ownership markets cannot even be simulated (see Mises 1951; Hanson 1989). Mises was certainly right in that private appropriability (including potential transferability and use/abuse) of at least a share of enterprise profits and capital gains must be essential to the very existence of entrepreneurship[9]; however this does not necessarily imply the private ownership of any of the actual means of production. In fact one could imagine a state ownership system in which state assets are leased on competitive leasing markets to private entrepreneurs, who appropriate at least part of any residual income and who by selling their leases to others, can realise the present value of their entrepreneurial activities, without ever acquiring ownership of capital goods or, technically, of any enterprise. In such a system investment could remain a state function, whose efficiency would be monitored by comparing, *ex post,* the return on investment obtained from the rentals determined in competitive leasing markets, to the interest rates prevailing at the time of investing.

It is tempting to conjecture that there can be no markets without private property, nor economic planning with private property: however this conjecture, though not rejected by experience, is still unproven on theoretical grounds. Once entrepreneurial rewards are at least partly appropriable it is possible to conceive a replication of competitive capital markets with or without the participation of private individuals but without private ownership of capital assets as such (see Nuti 1988 and 1989). These kinds of arrangements (which could be actual markets and not just simulations), however, are not a case against private ownership but a case for economic reform; ideological obstacles against reform could be side-stepped, even if they were not to disappear, as now seems the case. In practice leasings of state property (as in the Soviet "arenda" and the Polish "dzierzawa", and on an even larger scale in China) are one of the possible ways of implementing privatisation of state assets especially in special sectors such as agriculture, catering and small-scale production, but cannot represent a general exclusive alternative to the sale of assets and shares.

Another interesting question is whether entrepreneurship could be associated with forms of ownership other than state and private, such as municipal or co-operative. In the Soviet Union a great deal of emphasis has been placed on the growth of the co-operative sector, which in the 30 months since June 1987 has grown from 55 000 to 5.5 million employees (including members, full- and part-time dependent workers), and raised turnover from 29 million to 40 billion rubles. Soviet co-operatives are not subjected to the income and capital sharing restrictions typical of traditional co-operatives, and very often serve as shells for private enterprises. Therefore their growth is an indication of the potential role that might be played by ownership forms other than state or private under special conditions, but this growth cannot be taken at face value or simply extrapolated to other countries or periods. However it is conceivable that privatisation of state assets could help to transform dependent workers into partial entrepreneurs. This process seems to be making some progress in modern Western capitalism with the introduction of income and capital sharing and worker participation in enterprise decision-making (see Nuti 1990c).

General issues: subjectivisation

In the current privatisation experience of central and eastern European economies three general issues have arisen. The first is the danger that, in the early steps towards economic reform, decentralisation of decision-making from central bodies to enterprises might divest the state of its assets without transferring ownership rights to other subjects. In that case it is as if state ownership became "res nullius", and before privatisation can take place it is necessary to undertake and complete a process of "re-subjectivisation", re-uniting property rights under the same public holder before actually privatising. This is what happened in Hungary with the 1984-85 legislation on state enterprises, which de facto acquired most of the rights associated with ownership on the unprecedented and nonsensical theory that "enterprises belong to themselves" (as officially stated by the Ministry of Justice). This unusual state was not remedied by the first attempts at privatisation (Act VI 1988; Act XIII 1989; see Hare 1990).

A similar problem arises in those countries where workers have gained a measure of self-management: some of the new shares may have to be sold or granted to enterprise employees, in order to trade off their full management rights (incompatible with shareholders' rights) with fuller ownership rights on a smaller scale (therefore embodying a smaller voice in enterprise management). Regardless of this argument, or beyond the limits of this kind of "conversion", shares may be sold to workers in order to strengthen popular support and to promote a property-owning democracy as an alternative system. Forms of workers' ownership abound in a capitalist economy: Employee Stock Ownership Plans (ESOPs, where workers acquire shares held collectively before they are distributed after a period or at retirement or departure) or Trusts (ESOTs, where workers are temporary co-owners and only enjoy a share of the revenue while they are employed), Personal Equity Plans (for regular savers, attracting tax exemption up to a maximum limit), Equity Holding Cooperatives, additional Pension Funds, Swedish-type collective investors, and so forth (see Uvalic 1990).

The new shares can be partly managed by state holdings and new pension funds. State holdings – as noted above – are often regarded with suspicion, as bearers of central interests dependent on and ultimately answering to the centre. There is however no reason why they should not respond to a policy commitment to make profits instead of being responsible for the achievement of government targets (the Italian state holding IRI, for instance, has responded to policy changes and has rapidly turned from an endemic loss maker into a profit-oriented and profit-making entity, presiding over privatisation). Pension funds (new, for there are none in Eastern European economies) are also credible collective investors, but they should only be given as much stock as they can reasonably need to take over pension liabilities; there is no justification in profits funding the consumption of pensioner rentiers, instead of being channelled to self-financed investment.

It is conceivable that the banking system might exercise control over companies through direct and indirect (namely on behalf of clients) shareholdings and the associated voting rights. Such a role is typical of the German-Japanese model of financial markets and has been advocated for Poland by Gomulka (1989). However, banks in that model rely on a full-fledged stock exchange and do not replace it. Thus the ability of the banking system to hold and administer state ownership should not be overestimated[10].

Private appropriation of state property

A phenomenon often practised and sometimes advocated in our "transitional" economies is the private appropriation of state property, either as a public policy of free distribution or as the result of spontaneous, "wild" auto-appropriation (in Polish *"samouwlaszczenie"*).

It has been suggested (for instance by Attila Soos in Hungary, Dusan Triska in Czechoslovakia, Jan Szomburg and Janusz Lewandowski in Poland) that shares in state enterprises or holdings may be given away freely to all citizens, directly or in the form of vouchers. This policy seems to have the advantage of creating an instant capital market, as well as the political advantage of generating instant capitalism and popular support for it. The needs of budgetary balance and monetary discipline, however, should strictly limit any privileged access to shares, as well as their free distribution (apart from the need of "converting" self-management rights into ownership stakes, discussed in the previous section). Free distribution of shares would be costly [as it was in the only known case to date, in British Columbia in 1979][11]. It would add a wealth effect to consumption demand, worsening inflationary pressure whether open or repressed. It would have an urban bias (of a kind that would not be present in case of free distribution of the profits of state enterprises as citizens' income): peasants in remote rural areas would be unlikely to benefit as much as the inhabitants of the capital city. As soon as potential limits to disposal lapsed, free distribution would also likely lead to rapid retrading and concentration of assets in the hands of a few better-informed people with access to liquid means (if this is not a preoccupation, perhaps a lottery with large bundles of shares would be preferable and cheaper to administer). The state is not withering away in the course of transition and will continue to tax: "Daddy state... is alive and well", as Kornai (1990, p. 82) graphically puts it; privatisation revenues could replace taxes, thereby avoiding their distortionary effects on economic efficiency (Newbery 1990).

Free share issues are often advocated on grounds of lack of sufficient domestic capital. However – depending on the policy towards debt-equity swaps – domestic credit may be granted on a large scale for the population to take part in privatisation; as long as this credit is sterilised and is not recycled to government expenditure, it can create a useful buffer against possible subsequent loss of macroeconomic control, when the government might sell its credits rather than raise additional taxes. In a country like Poland, state revenue from privatisation could be used to retire hard currency credits of enterprises and households via the state banking system, which are not backed by hard currency reserves and therefore limit central control over the money supply. Finally, the free gift of state assets seems an out-of-place largess on the part of governments heavily indebted to international creditors, who would be justified in asserting a prior claim to those assets[12].

The other form of private appropriation – spontaneous, or "wild" auto-appropriation – is worse because it is selective: privatisation without publicity and competition may result at least partially in divestiture, rather than sale, and in the parallel appropriation of state property by a few well-informed people in positions of power. In the early stages of privatisation in Hungary and Poland (Hare 1990, Grosfeld 1990, Chilosi 1990), then elsewhere, managers and party officials often converted their position into a share of state capital, through semi-legal or outright illegal transactions tolerated because of their large scale and the offenders' positions. This type of transaction includes: subcontracting of profitable activities, reciprocal disposals between state enterprise managers to their personal advantage, personal deals in joint ventures with foreign partners, artificial liquidation of viable activities transferred to internal bidders, etc.[13]. There is no conceivable justification for condoning these practices, which are equivalent to the worst cases of insider trading in western markets.

Privatisation in the reform sequence

A crucial general question is the position of privatisation in the sequence of reform measures, i.e. whether it should occur during or after stabilisation, before or after de-monopolisation, and financial and productive restructuring.

It seems most inappropriate to sell off shares in state enterprises before stabilisation and fiscal reform. Here stabilisation is understood as domestic market equilibrium in non-hyperinflationary or excessively inflationary conditions, at uniform prices; fiscal reform is understood as the termination of *ex-post, ad hoc,* enterprise-specific taxes and subsidies levelling profitability throughout the economy. Without these prior achievements, trends in product and input prices and therefore enterprise profitability would be impossible to assess, and as a result assets would be underpriced and yet unattractive in conditions of uncertainty. Thus privatisation cannot really contribute directly to the stabilisation process (see Nuti 1990a and 1990b). An exception can be the privatisation of housing (where the stream of future services is directly consumed by the owner), small plots of land and small scale services (where future benefits are more strictly dependent on the owner-worker's effort supply). This kind of "small" privatisation can contribute to stabilisation.

The very announcement of a firm decision to proceed with privatisation on a clearly predetermined schedule and procedure can itself make a contribution to stabilisation (the opposite happened in the USSR announcement of future price increases destabilised domestic markets and aggravated shortages). The announcement can be particularly effective if it is followed by the issue of special bonds, at low or zero nominal interest but carrying an option to purchase without restriction any state asset which will be privatised subsequently – pending the determination of asset prices. In Poland in November 1989 this instrument was used but bonds redeemable through privatisation were indexed and the timing and pattern of privatisation were not specified; thus the bonds cost the government much more than other forms of bond financing and even so, in the uncertainty about privatisation terms, were not very attractive to the public at the time of issue[14].

De-monopolisation is also a necessary precondition of privatisation: without it asset prices would include a capitalisation of monopoly power, which would be either unduly validated or – from the viewpoint of buyers – unfairly removed later on. A firm commitment to subsequent de-monopolisation still leaves a strong element of uncertainty; foreign trade liberalisation may alleviate the problem by raising the degree of competition.

The transformation of state enterprises into joint stock companies presupposes the valuation of their net assets and their recapitalisation (as the Czechs put it, "the bride has to be endowed before being given away..."). Or, if necessary, excess liquid resources may be drained away before privatisation; at least some rationalisation of output structure and input outlays (including labour employment) must take place. To proceed otherwise implies the likely underselling of state assets. If, before privatisation, an active capital market has been organised, valuation and financial restructuring can be left to competitive mechanisms; otherwise some competitive redeployment of assets has to be stimulated among state enterprises. In any case it seems important that labour redundancies and redeployments should be handled before, rather than after, privatisation, both to ensure fair compensation of workers and to make assets more attractive to potential alternative users.

The Polish economic framework

In the ten years preceding 1990 Poland experienced stagnation in real output, while consumption levels fell by 10 per cent over the ten years to end-1989). Polish external debt reached $42 billion (of which $28 billion was owed to other governments), too large an amount to be fully serviced in spite of recurring trade surpluses (about $1 billion per year in 1985-89). Shortages were endemic and inflation accelerated reaching the yearly rate of 740 per cent in 1989, when output declined by 1.7 per cent (see Kolodko 1989).

The economic framework of the 1990 drive towards privatisation is that of a drastic stabilisation programme, launched by the new Mazowiecki Government on 1 January 1990, aimed at restoring market equilibrium, introducing resident convertibility for current transactions, and promoting net exports, while at the same time making progress towards reform and restructuring (see Kolodko 1990, Frydman-Kolodko-Wellisz 1990, Nuti 1990c).

The stabilisation package envisaged the abolition of subsidies and the reduction of the budget deficit to 1 per cent of GNP (down from 8 per cent in the previous year); monetary discipline and an increase in real interest rates to positive levels (the interest rate was raised also on old contracts, amounting to a tax); almost complete price liberalisation (except for energy, pharmaceuticals and fertilisers, whose price increases were diluted in subsequent months); very mild wage indexation of wage guidelines (at 30 per cent of inflation in January, 20 per cent in February to April, 60 per cent in May to December except for July when indexation was 100 per cent to compensate for energy price increases) and penal taxation over that level; trade liberalisation; 32 per cent devaluation of the zloty, made convertible and held at 9 500 zlotys per dollar, with the backing of external assistance provided by international agencies and the Group of 24 (a $700 million International Monetary Fund (IMF) stand-by credit, a $1 billion stabilisation fund, $300 million from the World Bank, EC-coordinated assistance under the PHARE programme, and credits and gifts by individual countries) and the rescheduling of debt service.

The programme was successful in establishing domestic market equilibrium: net exports rose to $1.7 billion over the first seven months; inflation exploded going up to the monthly (point-to-point) rate of 105 per cent in January 1990 then settled down to 4-6 per cent per month, which is still much too high on a yearly basis; and the exchange rate was held at the target rate, in spite of hyperinflation and continued inflation differentials with hard currency countries (which just goes to show how grossly undervalued it must have been in January 1990). However, the real purchasing power of wages (formerly overestimated by statistics because of permanent shortages) fell by a third; output in mid-year stagnated after a fall of over one-third; and unemployment, around 10 000 at the end of 1989, grew fast and at the end of July 1990 had reached 700 000, rising at a rate of over 25 000 per week – government forecasts expect 1.3 million unemployed by the end of 1990.

In brief, the stabilisation programme has overshot its output, employment and real wages targets, and yet there is hardly a sign of "supply response". Against this background the advantages expected of privatisation – demand deflation, efficiency, entrepreneurship – become particularly important.

Polish privatisation: debates and practice

In Poland there is a long standing tradition of private enterprise both in agriculture (following the de-collectivisation of 1956, with about 4 million employees today) and outside agriculture as well, especially in the last six years (private manufacturing, transport and other services, including joint ventures, with over 1 million employees). This makes up almost one-third of the labour force, and grew in 1988 at 11 per cent while state employment was falling at 1-2 per cent; these trends have accelerated in 1989-90. By early 1990 there were 845 677 private enterprises (though mostly of very small size) attracting the best employees away from the public sector (Chilosi 1990). Official forecasts for 1990 expect state industrial output to fall by 28 per cent and private output to grow by 5 per cent, bringing the relative shares of the two sectors in industry from 92 to 87-88 per cent and from 8 to 12-13 per cent, respectively.

The privatisation of Polish state assets and the setting up of a stock exchange where they could be sold and retraded were already under consideration by the last communist-dominated Polish Government, and naturally were revamped by the Mazowiecki-led coalition (see Grosfeld 1990). Finance Minister Leszek Balcerowicz, speaking at the IMF assembly in Washington in October 1989, stated that:"The Government of Poland intends to transform the Polish economy to a market economy. This process is to be accompanied by a gradual change in the pattern of ownership towards that which prevails in countries with advanced economies."

Privatisation has been generally regarded as a deflationary instrument to avoid or reduce hyperinflation, a guarantee of enterprise independence from central organs and, most importantly, a way of enhancing productivity and entrepreneurship.

The main difficulty faced by both the former and the present government has been the reconciliation of privatisation schemes with the self-management institutions set up in Polish enterprises by the legislation of September 1981 (see Nuti 1981 for a comparison of the legislation with the more militant draft law submitted by Solidarity at that time). This legislation gave workers collectively some, indeed most, of the rights usually exercised by shareholders (such as managerial appointments and dismissals, verification of current performance, distribution of profit, and investment plans). Therefore the transformation of state enterprises into joint stock companies to be sold off to the public implies the cancellation or substantial dilution of those rights which, especially at times of drastic reductions in real wages, has to be compensated and negotiated. But there were also other difficulties, in part indirectly related to the modification of self-management.

The starting position of workers before privatisation is that of part entrepreneurs – not having ownership rights but having extensive decision-making rights and some profit-related benefits – for 100 per cent of the enterprise. An obvious trade off is that of giving workers the position of full entrepreneurs – i.e. 100 per cent owners, decision-makers and residual claimants – as shareholders in the enterprise with a much smaller stake. But how much smaller? And should it not be an equal absolute stake in all enterprises rather than a percentage which would unduly favour capital-intensive sectors? But then how are shares to be valued, before a capital stock is set up? Should one start with the ailing enterprises or with the viable ones? And why limit the share-out to workers in state enterprises, excluding for instance workers in government services, or the unemployed; should everybody not have an equal share of state assets financed by past consumption sacrifices on the part of the whole population? Current savings could not afford to buy more than a small fraction of the whole national capital anyway. Why not give everybody a free share in all state enterprises, or rather in a number of state holding companies, thus solving at a stroke problems of capital valuation, equality and small size of the market? Or perhaps free equal vouchers should be offered to the whole adult population to convert into a portfolio of their choice as privatisation proceeds. But then, why dilapidate state assets when the state budget deficit must be eliminated and there are pressing welfare needs, not to speak of the burden of external debt? Should sales and debt-equity swaps not be explored first? Could workers in state enterprises be satisfied by a combination of lesser involvement in decision-making and stronger participation in enterprise profit, instead of having to be paid off with a capital stake?

These questions were hotly debated in Poland and arguments somewhat impeded the progress of privatisation.

The new Polish law on privatisation (July 1990)

The office of the Government Plenipotentiary for questions of Property Transformations – a new ministerial post in the new government, held by Krzystof Lis – prepared a number of successive versions of draft laws on "The Privatisation of State Enterprises" and on "The Council of National Capital and the Agency for Ownership Transformations" (Biuro 1990a and 1990b). In April 1990 the 15th version was presented to the Polish Parliament, with a counter-draft law being submitted by a group of Trade Union deputies close to Andrzej Milkowski of OKP (Solidarity's Citizen Parliamentary Committee; see OKP 1990). The government project, somewhat modified to take into account suggested amendments, was approved in July 1990 by impressive majorities (328 votes to two with 39 abstentions in the lower house; 60 votes to seven with two abstentions in the Senate), but it left many issues still unresolved.

The Law establishes a Ministry of Property Transformation, to oversee the transformation of state enterprises into share companies initially held by the Treasury as single shareholder, followed within two years by the sale of shares to domestic and foreign investors, mostly by public offer at a prefixed price. The initiative to privatise a given enterprise can be taken by management, workers or the "founding organs" (i.e. the central body or bodies exercising authority on the enterprise to date) and is subject to governmental authorisation.

Up to 20 per cent of shares are reserved for workers of the privatised enterprise at a 50 per cent discount on the price of issue; the discount however cannot exceed half of the buyer's salary over the last six months. This is an ingenious constraint which broadly equalises access to capital by employees in enterprises characterised by different amounts of capital per person.

This reserve creates a potential class of 4 million small investors but excludes from the discount the other 13 million working in state agencies other than enterprises and in the private sector; however a portion (expected to be 10-20 per cent) of the shares of companies undertaking privatisation is to be distributed freely and equally to the general public. Moreover, access to capital ownership is facilitated by the fact that shares can be purchased on credit, if so decided by the Minister of Property Transformation and the Minister of Finance. In order to limit *nomenklatura* acquisitions only individuals can acquire shares at the time of privatisation. As long as an enterprise is in state hands, one-third of the board of directors is to be elected by workers.

Foreign investors can freely purchase state company shares subject to an overall ceiling of 10 per cent, which can be raised by the Agency for Foreign Investments (transferred to the Ministry of Property Transformations from the Foreign Trade Ministry). Dividends and the proceeds of subsequent share sales may be repatriated abroad without special permits.

An alternative form of ownership transformation is through liquidation, i.e. selling or leasing all or part of the enterprise assets to employees or external entrepreneurial groups, preferably at public auction, with a view to facilitate the creation of new private enterprises.

Several hundred enterprises are expected to close in the next year, and their assets will be sold or leased. Privatisation of some companies (out of over 7 000 potential candidates) started in September 1990; some leading enterprises will be included, e.g. the Kielce construction conglomerate Exbud and a cable factory in Czechowice. Foreign assistance is providing funds to pay the fees of Western consultants and banks involved in this operation.

Opposition to earlier government plans had been voiced primarily on the grounds of infringement of workers' self-management rights, neglect of workers' ownership schemes and excessive concentration of power in the hands of the CNC President. The proposed counter-project left greater scope for ESOP-type schemes of employee ownership and for access to finance by domestic investors, and envisaged greater social control over privatisation, at the risk however of bureaucratising the process. The Law approved in July 1990 made some concessions in this direction, introducing some free shares and the possibility of purchases on credit.

A central question remains: what role foreign capital might play in Polish privatisation, and therefore the weight of implicit or explicit "debt-equity swaps". Capital inflows to date have been fairly small (a cumulative amount of $200 million to March 1990 for joint ventures – over one-third from West Germany – compared with a Soviet total of $600 million). On the one hand foreign participants are needed to secure competition, to provide know how and fresh hard currency capital; on the other hand Poland has little incentive to repay the extant debt ($41.4 billion at end-1989, or 4.8 times total Polish yearly exports) out of national capital assets, other than as part of an international exercise in debt relief or at a discount comparable to that at which Polish commercial debt retrades today in secondary markets (over 80 per cent). In any case, the result of any privatisation targeted to foreign buyers is indeterminate without stipulating the associated credit policy (determining the zloty credit available to domestic buyers for the purchase of state assets) and exchange rate policy (determining the domestic value of foreign bids).

The Law leaves to governmental discretion the scale and time schedule of privatisation; Parliament is to set only "basic directions" for privatisation once a year and decides on the uses to which sales revenues are to be put. The law also leaves to future governmental decisions the scale of free distribution, the scale of credit sales and the size of foreign acquisitions; it also leaves to subsequent legislation the institution and regulation of financial markets – a step which is obviously out of sequence. Until these questions are resolved, the progress of privatisation is bound to continue to be controversial and to be delayed.

Notes

1. According to Strumilin, a sufficient condition of full communism is that free consumption should be the larger share. However in order to measure the relative shares of free and non-free goods – unless all goods are subject to a two-tier (free and non-free) regime – it is necessary to use a set of weights, i.e. actual or shadow prices. Yet it is not clear from where the necessary price system would come. In principle prices could come from a system of marginal valuations with reference to a central body, were it not for the fact that under full communism presumably central bodies "wither away" with the state.

2. If I consume a quantity $c(i)$ of good i per unit of time and that good has durability $T(i)$, I can carry a revolving stock of $c(i)*T(i)$; if $v(i)$ is the storage volume required per unit of of consumption good i and I have a maximum storage space V, then I will have a maximum command on a stock of consumption goods given by a vector c with elements $c(i)*T(i)$ subject to the scalar product of c and v (the corresponding vector of storage requirements per unit of consumption) being equal to or less than V. Here "durability" means 100 per cent conservation for a period of time $T(i)$, which is equivalent to a zero real own rate of return on storage; this already gives rise to an optimisation problem, in that the rational consumer, given his expected future claims to consumption $c(i, t)$ will equate his real rate of time preference, implicit in his rate of intertemporal substitution, to the zero own rate of return on storage. As a result of this maximisation problem actual stocks of goods $C(i, t)$ may well be lower than the maximum allowed by storage space and durability characteristics. In practice the consumption goods stored have a rate of decay $d(i)$ which is a function of storage time, i.e. $d(i)=d[i, T(i)]$, giving rise to a more complex optimisation problem, simultaneously determining $d(i)$ and $T(i)$ as well as $C(i, t)$; now there can be different real rates of time preferences for each good, being equated to the rate of decay which is an implicit negative rate of (own) real interest.

3. Even paper money could be made perishable if an early enough date were fixed by which it had to be spent, or its liquidity could be reduced if its validity as legal tender were subject to some inconvenient procedure of official validation. Keynes (1936), for instance, suggested that cash should be stamped at frequent intervals; for a history of the idea of money "melting" or "reabsorbing", see Morley-Fletcher (1980-81).

4. This cost is virtually equal to zero, or a small amount taken with a negative sign; if interest-earning liquid deposits are possible, they are treated here as financial assets different from money.

5. Except for contracts involving the delivery of future labour services, which would not be capitalistic but feudal, as they would imply the compulsory subjection of individuals to other individuals or firms.

6. China appears to have been an exception, at least until recently.

7. The March 1990 Soviet legislation on property prohibits one-man-owned enterprises employing wage labour, but allows joint-stock companies, somehow regarded as "collective" forms of ownership. This is an absurd distinction, co-ownership being no less private than one-man ownership of a whole asset. Soviet legislators literally are preventing

"exploitation of man" by one other man but allow it when it is done by several men together.

8. In the Soviet economy in 1990 excess liquid assets in the hands of the population are estimated, to be of the order of an average four months' wage bill; enterprises' inventories were 82 per cent of national income in 1985, compared with 31 per cent in the United States (Shmelev and Popov 1989, p. 305).

9. In this respect my own views have radically altered with respect to Nuti (1974), where the possibility of group entrepreneurship in the traditional socialist model was considered with excessive optimism.

10. Gomulka envisages a special role for banks in the privatisation process: public shareholdings in state enterprises would be entrusted to the management of banks, which would earn a share of dividends and realised capital gains; Gomulka regards privatisation of those banks as equivalent to the privatisation of the public assets entrusted to them but this is a misconception: if I buy shares in Merrill Lynch I do not acquire a stake in the portfolio of their clients. Moreover, emphasis on realised capital gains rather than on the increase of portfolio evaluation is bound to unduly inflate turnover (by encouraging a special case of so-called "bed and breakfast" transactions, i.e. sales followed by quick repurchases).

11. In early 1979 the provincial government of British Columbia set up a new Crown Corporation, the British Columbia Resources Investment Corporation, with $151.5 million in assets, and distributed five free shares to any citizen who asked for them, plus additional shares at $6 each; 170 000 persons were involved. However the new company made some bad investments and soon incurred substantial losses; the operation is not judged to have been a success (see Stanbury 1989, pp. 282-283).

12. The loss of potential collateral on the part of creditors may be thought to be overcompensated by the greater potential productivity which could derive from privatisation and the further impulse to economic reform. Certainly no international creditor has publicly argued against free distribution of state assets in debtor countries.

13. The auto-appropriation of state assets by the nomenklatura has been facilitated in Poland by the extraordinary growth of joint stock and limited liability companies founded in Poland, which were almost 30 000 in 1989. Some transactions, in which managers appeared on both sides as sellers on behalf of their state enterprises and as buyers for their own companies or even joint ventures – naturally have been declared void by the Supreme Court, but the bulk of this kind of transaction are unlikely to be challenged especially when foreign buyers are also involved (Chilosi 1990).

    A famous case is that of Igloopol, the largest Polish agro-industrial complex, valued at 145 billion zlotys and artificially liquidated and transferred for 55 billion zlotys to a joint stock company with the same board of directors, whose shares - transferable at their discretion -were sold mostly to Party organisations and activists. The Ministry of Agriculture (of which the Igloopol Managing Director was Deputy Minister) approved the liquidation procedure in spite of a Ministry of Finance report which declared it illegal and economically unjustified (Grosfeld 1990). A recent decree of the Mazowiecki Government has now made illegal the participation of state enterprise managers and workers' councils in the companies founded by their own enterprise (Chilosi 1990).

14. Kolodko (1990) reports that a million zlotys invested in these bonds at the end of 1989 were worth by the end of the first quarter of 1990 2.5 million zlotys, compared with 1.3 million zlotys if invested in three-month deposits at the National Savings Bank (PKO) and 1.06 million zlotys if invested in dollar-denominated deposits. This is an indication of the lack of credibility of government policies.

References

ACT VI (1988) on *Economic Associations* [companies], HungaroPress, Special issue, October, Budapest.

ACT XIII (1989) on the *Transformation of Organizations carrying on economic activity and Economic Associations*, June, Budapest.

ASLUND, Anders (1985), *Private enterprise in Eastern Europe*, MacMillan, London.

BALCEROWICZ, Leszek (1989), *"Economic reforms in Poland and the role of financial aid"*, Ministry of Finance, Warsaw (mimeographed).

BIURO Pelnomocnika Rzadu do Spraw Przeksztalcen Wlasnosciowych (1990a), "Zalozenia rzadowego programu prywatyzacji przedsiebiorstw panstwowych", Warsaw.

BIURO Pelnomocnika Rzadu do Spraw Przeksztalcen Wlasnosciowych (1990b), Ustawa (Projekt) o prywatyzacji przedsiebiorstw panstwowych, April, Warsaw.

CHILOSI, Alberto (1990), *"L'economia polacca tra stabilizzazione e trasformazione istituzionale"*, Conference Paper, Pisa.

FRYDMAN, Roman, Grzegorz W. KOLODKO and Stanislaw WELLISZ (1990), *"Stabilisation in Poland: a Progress Report"*, Second International Monetary Conference, FU and Landeszentralbank Berlin, Berlin, 10-12 May.

GOMULKA, Stanislaw (1989), *"How to create a capital market in a socialist country and how to use it for the purpose of changing the system of ownership"*, Conference paper, LSE Financial Markets Group, 13 December.

GROSFELD, Irena (1990, "Prospects for privatisation in Poland", *European Economy No.43*, CEC Brussels, March.

HANSON, Phil (1989), "Von Mises' revenge", paper for the *Conference on Perestroika: a socioeconomic survey*, Radio Free Europe/Radio Liberty, Munich, 7-10 July.

HARE, Paul G. (1989), *"Reform of enterprise regulation in Hungary - from 'tutelage' to market"*, Seminar Paper, PHARE Group, EC-DG-II, Brussels, November.

HEMMING, Richard and Ali M. Mansoor (1988), "Privatisation and Public Enterprise", *IMF Occasional Paper No. 56*, Washington, D.C., January.

KEYNES, J.M. (1936), *The General theory of employment, interest and money*, London.

KOLODKO, Grzegorz W. (1989), "Reform, stabilisation policies, and economic adjustment in Poland", *WIDER Working Papers No.51*, Helsinki, January.

KOLODKO, Grzegorz W. (1990), "Polish hyperinflation and stabilisation 1989-1990", *Working Papers of the Institute of Finance No.10*, Warsaw.

KORNAI, Janos (1990), *The Road to a Free Economy – Shifting from a Socialist System: the Example of Hungary*, W.W. Norton & Co., New York and London.

MACAVOY, Paul W., *et al.* (1989), *Privatisation and state owned enterprises*, Kluwer Academic Publishers, Boston.

MEADE, James (1989), *Agathotopia: the economics of partnership*, The Hume Institute, London.

MISES, Ludwig von (1951), *Socialism – an economic and sociological analysis*, translated by J. Kahane, Liberty Classics, Indianapolis.

MORLEY-FLETCHER, Edwin (1980-81), "Per una storia dell'idea di 'minimo sociale garantito'", *Rivista Trimestrale, Nos.64-66*, October-March, pp. 297-321.

NEWBERY, David M. (199), *"Reform in Hungary: sequencing and privatisation"*. Paper presented at the EEA Fifth Annual Conference, Lisbon, September.

NUTI, D. Mario (1974), "Socialism and ownership", *The Socialist Idea*, eds. L. Kolakowski and S. Hampshire. Proceedings of a Conference at Reading University, 1973, Weidenfeld and Nicholson, London.

NUTI, D. Mario (1981), "Poland: socialist renewal and economic collapse", *New Left Review*, November.

NUTI, D. Mario (1988), "Competitive valuation and efficiency of capital investment in the socialist economy", *European Economic Review 32*, pp. 2-6.

NUTI, D. Mario (1989), "Feasible financial innovation under market socialism", eds. Christine Kessides, Timothy King, Mario Nuti, Kathy Sokil, *Financial Reform in Centrally Planned Economies*, EDI-World Bank, Washington, p. 6.1-6.31.

NUTI, D. Mario "Internal and international implications of monetary disequilibrium in Poland", *European Economy No.43*, March 1990a, CEC Brussels, pp. 169-182.

NUTI, D. Mario (1990b), "Stabilisation and reform sequencing in the Soviet Economy", *Recherches Economiques de Louvain, Vol.56*, No.2, pp. 1-12.

NUTI, D. Mario (1990c), "Alternative employment and payment systems", forthcoming in a DG-V volume on Profit-sharing, Commission of European Communities, Brussels.

OKP (1990), Kontr-Ustawa (Projekt) o przeksztalceniach wlasnosciowych przedsiebiorstw panstwowych, Warsaw. Polish Ministry of Finances, "Holding companies as a means of accelerating privatisation in Poland", Warsaw, 7 March.

SAPPINGTON, D., and J.E. Stiglitz (1987), "Privatisation, information, and incentives", *Journal of Policy Analysis and Management*, Vol.6, No.4, pp. 567-82.

SHMELEV, Nikolai and Vladimir Popov (1989), *The turning point: revitalising the Soviet economy*, Doubleday, New York.

STANBURY, W.T. (1989), *"Privatisation in Canada: ideology, symbolism or substance?"* , in MacAvoy *et al.*, pp. 272-329.

STIGLITZ, Joseph E. (1989), "On the economic role of the state", in Stiglitz et al., *The Economic Role of the State*, Blackwell, Oxford.

UVALIC, Milica (1990), *The PEPPER Report: Promotion of Employee Participation in Profits and Enterprise Results in the Member States of the European Community*, EUI and CEC, Florence and Brussels.

VICKERS, John and George YARROW (1988), *Privatisation: an economic analysis*, The MIT Press, Cambridge, Mass.

Property Rights Reform:
Hungarian Country Study

Keith Crane

Introduction

Before the collapse of the one-party state in 1989, the Hungarian authorities spent two decades attempting to implement a market-oriented economic reform. Despite some improvements on the centrally-planned system, these reforms failed to diminish the gap between Hungarian economic performance and that of the capitalist countries of Western Europe. With the advent of the new democratic political system, policy-makers have turned to the problem of creating a market economy.

The Hungarian Government has introduced several of the necessary initial measures to transform the economy: replacement of price controls and the concomitant administrative allocation of resources with markets, establishing the legal equivalence of private and state property, and the liberalisation of trade. Despite concerns about unemployment, foreign economic domination and the potential for some individuals to enrich themselves at the expense of the state, there is an emerging consensus in Hungary that the government must now take the second step towards the establishment of a market economy: the transfer of state-owned assets to the private sector. Hungarian economists have found that despite efforts by the government to impose cash restraints on state-owned firms and tie managerial evaluations to profitability, the perversities of the system lead managers away from profit maximisation or even cost minimisation. They have concluded that political pressures and ill-devised managerial incentives condemn state-owned enterprises to perform substantially worse than privately-owned firms. The solution to this problem is to greatly reduce the size of the state-owned sector in the economy.

Much of the shift from state to private ownership will be caused by market forces. New private businesses will grow and constitute a larger share of output. Those private businesses that are more efficient than state-run enterprises will crowd out their state-owned competitors. These processes will take time, however. In the interim most assets in Hungary are owned by the state. To the extent that these assets would be more efficiently utilised in the private sector, Hungary would greatly benefit, if these assets are transferred to private ownership. Although not a necessary condition for the emergence of a market economy in Hungary, the new Hungarian Government and the opposition parties believe that the country would benefit if state-owned industrial enterprises were to be privatised rather than left to wither in the face of competition from new private competitors.

Privatisation is likely to be a difficult process. Because the bulk of Hungarian assets have been held by the state, household assets are worth far less than either the replacement value or the value of the stream of discounted profits likely to be generated by Hungarian enterprises. Thus, the government faces the conundrum of whether to transfer rather than sell some of the assets to the household sector, encourage foreign buyers to purchase Hungarian firms, or keep the pace of asset sales such that enterprises do not have to be sold at a deep discount.

A second problem is the mechanics of sale. The government must develop policies on modes of sale, dissemination of information about enterprises to potential buyers, checks on fraud, etc. Widespread problems with fraud have already made privatisation an explosive political issue.

This paper assesses the prospects for the successful privatisation of state-owned assets in Hungary. It attempts to answer three questions:

i) What are the economic policy reasons for privatising state-owned industries in Hungary?

ii) How is privatisation likely to be carried out?

iii) What are the likely economic effects of privatisation?

Although some state-owned enterprises have been sold in whole or in part, Hungary is only in the first stages of privatisation. The legal framework is still being put in place and many sharply debated issues have yet to be resolved. Moreover, it is still far too early to tell if privatisation is producing the anticipated economic results. Consequently, the focus of this paper is on analysing the theoretical problems of privatisation and the theoretical validity of the various policy positions on privatisation. The discussion of the likely economic consequences of privatisation also draws on theory as well as the initial experiences of those firms that have already been privatised.

Why privatise?

A remarkable consensus has emerged in Hungary during the past year that assets in the socialist sector (state-owned enterprises and co-operatives) need to be transferred to the private sector. To an outsider this emphasis on private ownership is the most puzzling of the transformations in central and eastern Europe. Queues, wage controls, shoddy goods and curbs on travel are obviously unpopular phenomena, but the transfer of property from the state or local collectives to private citizens, some of whom will benefit substantially more than others, flies in the face of over four decades of emphasis on collective ownership and the rights of workers (admittedly little honoured in practice). However, the Hungarian populace has concluded that the former economic system has been a failure; Western capitalism is a successful system. If Hungary is to become a Western market economy, they argue, it must transfer assets from state to private ownership.

Less surprising has been the divergence of views among the parties represented in the Hungarian parliament concerning the speed and manner through which state-owned assets are to be sold to the private sector. The opposition, headed by the Free Democrats, has generally argued that state-owned property needs to be privatised quickly, even at the cost of obtaining lower proceeds from asset sales than would be available at a more leisurely pace. The Hungarian Democratic Forum, the leading party in the ruling coalition, has argued that the process should proceed more deliberately so as to maximise revenues from asset sales. A second member of the ruling coalition, the Smallholders Party, has sought to cut the Gordian knot by restoring all property to the owners as of 1947. Although this scheme seems infeasible, its popularity among some voters illustrates the difficulties the new Hungarian Government faces in attempting to establish a policy on privatisation.

These competing approaches to privatisation rely on differing theoretical arguments over why privatisation is necessary and its likely consequences. For this reason, this first section reviews the rationales for privatisation and provides a critical assessment of the various arguments.

The capital efficiency argument

One argument on which all parties concur is that Hungarian state-owned industry uses and invests capital much less efficiently than private industry in market economies. If the use of capital and investment decisions are transferred from the state to private individuals, Hungary as a whole will benefit because of substantial increases in capital productivity.

The evidence in favour of this argument, in contrast to some others used to support privatisation, is overwhelming. Even in comparison with other countries in central and eastern Europe, Hungary has performed near the bottom in terms of increasing capital efficiency[2]. Although Hungary has outperformed Czechoslovakia, Poland and, by some measures, eastern Germany (German Democratic Republic before the unification of Germany) in terms of total factor productivity growth, changes in capital productivity, with the exception of Poland, have been worse (Table 1). These three countries are fairly similar to Hungary in terms of levels of economic development. None of them are known as economic success stories.

Hungary's poor performance is even more puzzling in light of the emphasis economic policy-makers have given improving economic efficiency since the introduction of the New Economic Mechanism (NEM) in 1968. Why has Hungary performed so poorly?

Part of this failure can be traced to ideological rigidities and mistaken assumptions. With the introduction of the 1968 reform policy-makers believed that

Table 1. **Comparative productivity growth in central and eastern Europe: 1968-85**

Average annual figures, %

	Czechoslovakia	Eastern Germany	Poland	Hungary
Changes in capital productivity	−1.42	−0.30	−2.16	−1.72
Changes in labour productivity	3.54	4.54	3.26	5.35
Changes in total factor productivity (eastern German weights)	2.23	3.26	2.01	3.47
Changes in total factor productivity (Hungarian weights)	1.23	2.28	0.80	2.04

71

substantial improvements in efficiency in input usage would be forthcoming by tying incentives to profits and introducing more rational prices. However, at least until the late 1970s, they still assumed that major investment decisions could be best made by the "centre".

The belief that the centre knows best is reflected in the allocation of investment. In the first two decades of the reform the central authorities were directly responsible for the allocation of over half of investment in industry. Enterprise managers were supposed to allocate the other half, primarily smaller investments at the factory level that would eliminate bottlenecks or improve quality. In practice, even these investment decisions were greatly influenced by the centre. Only 20-30 per cent of the 50 per cent of investments that were supposed to be determined by enterprise managers were financed by retained earnings. Roughly 20 per cent were financed by state grants and the rest by the national bank. Because the Central authorities had the overriding say in determining the allocation of grants and loans, they determined most of the investments even in areas nominally under enterprise control. In fact the 10-15 per cent of total investments determined solely by enterprise management was roughly equivalent to the share decided independently before the introduction of the reform[1].

Poor allocation of investment

Despite or because of its dominant role in the distribution of investment, the Hungarian Government has been remarkably inept in choosing where to allocate these funds. I have compared profitability with changes in the share of gross investment by industrial sector between the second half of the 1970s and the first half of the 1980s. The profitability ranking was constructed from a list of the largest 100 Hungarian enterprises ranked by rate of return published in 1987 *Figyelo,* a Hungarian business and news magazine[3].

The share of total investment of the least-profitable sectors tended to increase (Table 2). Machinery and chemicals (which includes pharmaceuticals) showed the best performance in terms of profitability; mining, metallurgy and electric power generation, the worst, yet investment shares moved in contrary directions. In fact, a

Table 2. **Distribution of Hungarian investment in industry**

	Shares of investment 1975-80 (per cent)	Shares of investment 1981-85 (per cent)	Difference	Sectoral Average of Firms' Profitability Ranking (1 to 100)
Mining	11.3	17.5	6.2	71.3
Electric energy	15.8	20.5	4.7	72.6
Metallurgy	9.0	8.1	−0.9	72.3
Machinery	18.4	15.0	−3.4	28.5
Construction materials	6.2	3.7	−2.5	49.3
Chemicals	15.1	15.4	0.3	28.1
Light industry	9.0	7.8	−1.2	41.2
Other industry	1.1	0.9	−0.2	44.7
Food industry	14.1	11.1	−3.0	55.8

Spearman Rank Order test on changes in investment shares and rankings by rate of return generated a positive correlation of .395, with a p-value of .2928, between the profitability ranking and the share of investment. In other words, industries with the best rates of return did not increase their shares of total investment, in fact they tended to see a decline.

Kornai and Matits have also found little relationship between profits and investments. They analysed the results of all state-owned enterprises between 1975 and 1982 and found no relationship between rate of return and profits and subsequent investment levels. They also found no relationship between investments and subsequent profits[4].

One major reason for the absence of a link between the two is the enormous role of the state in redistributing profits from profitable firms to lossmakers (Table 3).

Table 3. **Transition probabilities due to fiscal redistribution in the state sector of manufacturing in 1982**

From original Profitability	To final profitability			
	Loss Maker	Low Profitability	Medium Profitability	High Profitability
Loss maker	0.233	0.500	0.122	0.145
Low profitability	0.038	0.853	0.103	0.006
Medium profitability	0.000	0.734	0.206	0.060
High profitability	0.008	0.394	0.515	0.083

Note: "Transition" means the proportion of firms in any given original profitability class that became members of a given final profitability class as a result of fiscal redistribution. The transition from 'original" to "final" profitability means the transition from the pre-tax and pre-subsidy position to the post-tax and post-subsidy position.
Source: KORNAI (1986), p. 1697.

This diversion of funds was due to the desires of the central authorities to channel industrial development. It was also due to their unwillingness to close loss-making firms and the subsequent need to generate funds to support these enterprises. To preserve budgetary balance when subsidies became too great a drain on the treasury, the Finance Ministry frequently levied retroactive taxes and expropriated reserve and investment funds from enterprises. For example, despite a law forbidding the state to take capital from an enterprise, in 1983 the government took 27 million forints from the 45 million forint reserve fund of the Egyesult Vegyimuvek, levied taxes of 5 million forints on previously taxed income, and forced the enterprise to purchase government bonds with the remaining 13 million forints. In 1985 the enterprise director requested the bonds from the Ministry of Finance and was informed they had yet to be printed[5].

Why is the state so inept in choosing investments? Decisions on that half of investment determined directly by the central authorities were frequently determined by perceived needs or political criteria (regional development, CMEA obligations, favoured industrial sectors) rather than a thorough analysis of relative rates of return. The National Planning Office, in particular, frequently focused on creating production capacities that would satisfy administratively set quantity targets, rather

73

than choosing investments based on relative rates of return. This was partly an artefact of the Office's brief: assuring planned allocations match supplies. For example, when the Soviet Union notified the Hungarians that petroleum supplies would be restricted during the 1980-85 plan period Hungarian planners faced growing imbalances in the energy sector. Planners responded by investing in coal mines and nuclear energy with little regard to rates of return; they were fixated on increasing domestic energy output in order to eliminate the energy shortfall. Consequently, investments were diverted from sectors with higher rates of return and from convertible currency export producers to the mining and power generating sectors. The cost of this decision has been continuing declines in the capital/output ratio, little progress in energy conservation, as funds have been used to produce energy rather than to invest in energy conservation equipment, and continued loss of Hungary's share of OECD markets for manufactures as Hungarian products have failed to keep pace with the competition.

Enterprise managers frequently contributed to poor decisions by the state. Perverse investment behaviour at the enterprise level was induced by flaws in the New Economic Mechanism (NEM). Managers faced very strong incentives to invest. Pushed to increase output and exports and improve quality by their superiors in the branch ministries, managers viewed investment as the principle means for achieving these goals. They also faced few disincentives to invest. The central authorities provided a large share of investment funds in the form of grants or loans at concessionary interest rates so investment was relatively cheap. They also showed themselves willing to bail out enterprises experiencing difficulties repaying loans. Consequently, enterprises faced what Kornai calls a "soft budget constraint"; they did not suffer the financial consequences of poor investment decisions.

Because of the soft budget constraint, the government could not allocate investment funds through interest rates alone. Consequently, credit rationing was an important instrument for controlling the supply of money. Enterprises investing in areas favoured by the central authorities or that were deemed important by the authorities were granted credits; those that did not have these connections were denied them. Thus, projects offering higher rates of return might be refused credits, while well-placed enterprise managers were able to procure funding for investments promising lower rates of return.

Enterprise demand for investment was not infinite. Managers faced a budget constraint imposed by past profits, a portion of which were assigned to a development fund (60 per cent of amortisation also went into this fund) and their ability to obtain bank loans. Moreover, managers of loss-making enterprises tended to be dismissed, so managers also faced potential sanctions, if investments went awry.

The choice of investments at the enterprise level was also warped by the attempts by the central authorities to channel investments through central development programmes. In these programmes specific industries or product lines were targeted for development. Enterprises that were able to insert themselves in the programme were eligible for investment grants and bank credit. More importantly, they received priority in investment decisions, so when bottlenecks appeared in construction these enterprises had priority.

Fink (1983) has attempted to test the hypothesis that incentives at both the enterprise and the national level channelled investments into expanding capacities of existing enterprises rather than restructuring. He tests his model on Hungarian investment and output data between 1960 and 1980 and finds that investment is uncorrelated with either capital and machinery costs or output prices, but is highly correlated to increases in output in previous years. He argues that because factory managers were rewarded on the basis of enterprise size and for increasing output, investment was oriented towards expanding output rather than increasing economic efficiency. In other words, the existing structure of output was the primary determinant of the allocation of investment in the 1970s.

Poor utilisation of the existing capital stock

In general, Hungarian managers used existing capital stocks substantially less efficiently than their Western counterparts. The strongest evidence for this argument is that the average number of shifts in Hungarian industry was appreciably lower than in the West. Moreover even after the introduction of the reform, a "storming" mentality remained endemic to the system[6].

Hungarian enterprises maintained excess capital capacity so that sales targets could be reached at the end of each quarter and at the end of the year. This behaviour is readily apparent in Hungarian industrial output and trade figures which show surges at the end of each quarter (March, June, September, and an enormous surge in December.)

Second, due to the availability of low interest credits, the cost of capital for many enterprises was substantially lower than its shadow price, so managers frequently over-invested.

Poor capital utilisation is also explained by the phenomenon of "shortage." Enterprise managers frequently were forced to manufacture many components in-house (that a Western company would procure from a subcontractor) because they could not rely on domestic or CMEA suppliers and were forbidden to import the component from the West[7].

They generally produce these components in small series. In between production runs, the manufacturing equipment lay idle. If this capital could be transferred to private owners, Hungarian economists argue, it could quickly be turned to much more efficient uses, because the new owners would search out new markets so as to keep the equipment operating at capacity.

Privatisation of the nomenklatura

Curiously, one of the major rationales for privatisation is the disintegration of central control over enterprises. Enterprise managers, aware that their former reliance on contacts in the Hungarian Socialist Workers' Party will no longer assure them their positions, have attempted to use their inside knowledge and the fluid economic and political situation to buy out their enterprises at lower prices than would be likely if the enterprises were auctioned off. Some of these directors set up businesses on the side which treated the state-owned firm as a captive customer or supplier or bought out all or parts of the firm itself. Because *de facto* privatisation by enterprise managers and former party officials has spread so quickly, political parties have argued the state needs to step in firmly and dispose of state-owned assets quickly, so that enterprise managers do not usurp them.

One of the most famous attempts at this form of privatisation was a leveraged buy-out of the monopoly office supply retailer, APISZ, which was to be funded through Citicorp's partially owned subsidiary in Budapest. Popular outrage led to the collapse of the deal. This example has led to more cautious behaviour on the part of other would-be-managers-turned-owners. Public exposure has probably been the most effective policy instrument for minimising this type of sale.

The "Mining of Capital" argument

One argument for privatisation has been that the enterprise management in collusion with workers' councils are "mining" the enterprises of their capital. Managers and workers have, reportedly, been under much less strict state control during the past two years of political turmoil. They have responded by trying to feather their nests in the new situation by covering wage costs with depreciation allowances. Managers have been unwilling to oppose worker wage demands because their own futures are so uncertain and because of the increased importance of workers in the management of enterprises since the establishment of workers councils[9].

I have attempted to assess the plausibility of this behaviour by modelling the behaviour of managers. Managers derive a substantial share of their income from bonuses which are tied to profits. If one thinks of a manager as someone whose primary duty is to select the objective function of the enterprise, then managers should have attempted to maximise profits. Under this assumption and subject to the various constraints in the Hungarian economy, one would expect managers to attempt to utilise inputs so that the efficiency condition "marginal revenue product of input i equals the price of input is", is reached.

In 1985 the Hungarian authorities passed a law stipulating that enterprises establish either a workers' council, if the enterprise were large, or a workers assembly, if it were small. These bodies elect the director of the enterprise and vote on major issues concerning the firm. The councils have had a heavily managerial cast in practice. At the end of 1985, the first year in which they functioned, managers, economists, administrative workers or employees with technical backgrounds comprised four-fifths of council membership.

Theoretically, one could argue that a manager's income now depends most heavily on satisfying workers' demands because of the existence of workers' councils. If this is the case, managers might be attempting to maximise profits per worker. Under this model, the enterprise tends to employ more capital per worker than in the case of competitive markets. However, the model still does not predict workers would "mine" the capital stock[9].

Neither of these two models supports the contention that managers have an incentive to mine the capital stock. Other considerations also argue against such a conclusion. First, unemployment is rising in Hungary. Workers have more reason to fear for their jobs and more reason to wish to keep their current enterprise in operation. Managers also face greater insecurity of employment. If they drive their current enterprise into bankruptcy, they are highly unlikely to obtain a new position in the future. Thus, there seems to be little incentive for managers or workers to run their enterprise into the ground even during this period of transition.

Despite the prevalence of this argument[10], I could find little evidence that it has been a major problem. Investment has declined in Hungary.

It is not clear that enterprises are rechanneling investment funds into wages, however. The government has imposed a tight monetary and somewhat looser fiscal policy making it difficult for enterprises to invest. Central investments have been cut. These factors explain the declines in enterprise investments more convincingly than the "mining of capital" argument. Furthermore, the scandals surrounding privatisation have been caused by managers trying to buy state assets cheaply, not by managers running state-owned firms into the ground.

Conclusions

Of the economic arguments in favour of privatisation, the poor usage of the existing capital stock and abysmal performance of the Hungarian state in choosing investment projects stand out. The empirical and theoretical analyses indicate Hungarians would be much better off, if someone other than the state were making decisions on capital usage and investment. The expropriation of state-owned assets by enterprise managers and party officials is an argument for improving the way in which enterprises are sold. However, this problem has been used as much by proponents as opponents of privatisation. Proponents argue the only way to prevent managers from "expropriating" state assets appears to be to sell them to private investors who will be better able to control them. Finally, I could find little theoretical support for the notion that Hungarian managers and workers are consuming the national asset base. Neither the incentives nor the empirical evidence supports the contention that this is a widespread phenomenon that can only be countered by a rapid sale of state-owned assets.

How will Hungary privatise?

Many of the laws governing privatisation are already in place, passed by the former socialist government. However, the process of privatisation is governed not only by the laws, but also by the institutional arrangements and the policies pursued by the new government. Below I provide a brief discussion of the laws impinging on privatisation, the institutions involved in the process and the policies the new government is likely to pursue.

The legal framework

The law on business organisations

The key law governing privatisation is the Law on Business Organisations, passed 1 January 1989. The law newly regulates and codifies the creation and operation of business organisations such as small proprietorships, limited liability corporations and joint stock corporations. State-owned enterprises are now permitted to set up joint-stock companies either in the form of subsidiaries or in entirety. It was on the basis of this law that managers of state-owned enterprises began to transform their enterprises in preparation for privatisation. The law also opened up loopholes through which some of these managers attempted to purchase their enterprises at less than market value.

The law also makes it possible for private individuals to establish limited liability companies and joint stock companies for the first time since the late 1940s. It establishes the equivalence of private and state-owned firms thereby relaxing a number of strictures on private investment, especially on the number of employees a private enterprise could hire.

The law unleashed a flood of applications for the establishment of limited liability companies, over 2 598 by September 1989[11]. Most of these are small businesses whose primary owner wishes to convert from a sole proprietorship to a limited liability company. However, a number of state-owned enterprises have also begun to use this form of ownership.

The law on the transformation of enterprises

The Law on the Transformation of Enterprises, passed 30 May 1989, was in some ways an addendum to the Law on Business Organisations. It permitted state-owned enterprises to convert themselves into limited liability corporations more simply and at lower cost than was possibly before the passage of the law.

This law also permits the sale of stock to entities such as other corporations and commercial banks. The new commercial banks, especially, have taken equity stakes in companies and companies have taken equity stakes in the banks. The spate of joint ventures with Western firms are almost entirely joint stock companies. In many instances the parent company has entered in the new business in conjunction with other companies. The new company has issued stock and each of the participants have purchased a share with a corresponding right to the profits and capital of the new enterprise. Sales of stock to private individuals were prohibited initially, but are now permitted. Bonds, however, another new innovation, were sold to the public.

A good example of a state-enterprise that has converted to a joint stock company is Medicor, a medical supply company, one of Hungary's most successful enterprises, which has split itself into 10 companies. The parent enterprise became a holding company. Each subsidiary has at least 7 owners, although most (about 95 per cent) of each company's capital is held by the holding company. The parent plans to sell off 49 per cent of each subsidiary's stock over the next few years to raise capital. The enterprise director believed bank debt was too high and modernisation was essential; the current product line was not being modernised fast enough[12]. The enterprise needed an infusion of capital.

Despite the law, control over Hungarian enterprises remained unclear. According to the law, stock ownership determines who runs the company. However, joint stock companies have workers' councils which continue to have the right to vote on the enterprise plan and on the choice of director, thereby attenuating control by the legal proprietor. Some enterprises have attempted to surmount this problem by issuing a species of preferred stock to employees. The stock grants the holder a share of profits, but no voting rights, but also generates a closer link between employees and enterprise ownership.

78

The law on foreign investment in Hungary

Hungary has permitted joint ventures with Western firms since the early 1970s. However, it was only with the passage of the Law on Investment by Foreigners in Hungary on 1 January 1989 that foreign investment has become of any importance. The law gives foreign investors most of the same rights as Hungarian investors. It permits them to purchase up to 100 per cent of a Hungarian enterprise, state or private. It also permits the repatriation of capital and all profits in convertible currency and establishes tax holidays for foreign investors.

This law has been crucial for privatisation. Foreign investors are considered to be a major potential source of investment funds. They have been the largest purchasers of stock in Hungarian enterprises to this point. Foreign companies have the technological, managerial and marketing expertise needed to ease Hungary's transition to a market economy.

The only significant strictures on foreign investors involve the purchase and sale of land. Foreign investors are permitted to buy land through Hungarian-registered companies which they own. However, the companies can only purchase real estate needed to conduct the business activities laid down in their Statutes of Association. Furthermore, the company needs a special permit to buy real estate, if the real estate was not acquired from the Hungarian partner at the time of formation. Foreign owners are not permitted to buy and sell real estate as a part of their normal business activities nor are they permitted to own agricultural land.

The bankruptcy law

One of the first steps towards making privatisation feasible was the passage of the law on bankruptcy in September 1986, long before massive privatisation was contemplated as a policy. The law permitted creditors, not just the legal owner of an enterprise, formerly the ministry, to initiate bankruptcy proceedings. The law has been an important step in establishing a separate economic and legal identity for enterprises, divorced from the state.

Despite the passage of the law creditors have been reluctant to initiate bankruptcy proceedings because they have been afraid the authorities will look on them with disfavour and may retaliate against them in the future. Moreover, once proceedings have been initiated, loans made to the bankrupt company have been considered uncollectable and have to be deducted from the creditor company's profits, thereby reducing management bonuses and workers' wage raises. Many firms are dependent on troubled firms for supplies or sales. If the supplier goes bankrupt, in Hungary's quota-filled economy the creditor could face serious problems importing the lost inputs from other sources, because it could not obtain the necessary import permits. In most cases alternative domestic suppliers did not exist. The government has also been reluctant to initiate proceedings because it is then called upon to provide support for restructuring.

The law on safeguarding of state assets

The latest major pieces of legislation affecting privatisation were the Law on Safeguarding State Assets and the Law on the State Assets Fund and the Administration and Utilisation of its Assets, both passed in 1990. Initial drafts of these bills were adopted by the Council of Ministers in 1989, but were further revised in January 1990 in discussions with the emerging political parties and concerned groups[13]. The laws were adopted in part to clarify control over state-owned assets. They were primarily motivated by a desire to assure that the state obtain fair value from sales of state-owned property and to prevent enterprise managers, purchasers or government officials from taking advantage of property sales for their personal gain. Hungarian lawmakers were also concerned that Hungary's reputation was suffering among serious investors because companies were being sold on the basis of personal contacts, not openly, on the basis of competitive bidding. Invitations for competitive bidding were rare and competitors offering a higher price were often excluded from the bidding.

This state of affairs was made possible because of the political alliance which evolved between politicians and large enterprise managers over the past few decades. Enterprise managers were heavily represented on the Central Committee of the Hungarian Socialist Workers' Party and in the Parliament. In part because of their increased autonomy under the NEM and because of their political clout, state enterprise managers had as much internal decision-making authority with regard to property as did the Politburo. Managers were generally the people who sold state property.

Since many large state-owned enterprises faced severe financial problems which could be ascribed to poor management, managers rightly felt threatened about an impending change in ownership. Not surprisingly, managers frequently sold enterprises at low prices in exchange for higher income and job tenure. Thus they became beholden to the new owners rather than to the state.

The laws establish professional control over privatisation implemented by enterprises and provide for the representation of the interests of the state as owner during privatisation. They were not designed to stop enterprises from creating joint stock companies or to usurp powers previously granted the enterprise[14]. However, they make the process of privatisation into a transparent, socially acceptable and controlled framework and give Parliament a greater say. The law also makes it mandatory to appraise property independently before sale. Property appraisal has been poor.

The law was also designed to mitigate anti-entrepreneurial and anti-management moods within the country which had gained strength because of the scandals. These tendencies had also increased opposition to foreign investment and led to the rise of economic nationalism. Moreover, Hungary's credibility as a location for foreign investment declines as promises made by managers to foreign investors could not be kept because managers were operating outside the law. Another concern has been that Hungarian enterprises have become bargains for foreign investors because of the country's solvency problems.

The institutional framework

The commercial banking system

In 1987 Hungary began to create a commercial banking system. The functions of the National Bank of Hungary, a monopoly bank, were divided among several new commercial banks and a single, money-issuing central bank. The new commercial banks were expected to assess enterprise investment plans with an eye to expected rates of return and the central bank was to control monetary policy. The commercial banks may be joint stock companies owned by enterprises and the central bank or directly controlled by the central government. More recently, private individuals and foreign investors have been permitted to buy shares. Although the new banking system is substantially different from the monopoly bank characteristic of most other centrally-planned economies, the new banks have frequently taken into consideration factors other than risk and rate of return in their decisions for loans. However, during their first year of operation the banks took a much harder-nosed attitude towards loss-making enterprises than the old monopoly bank did[15].

Bond and stock markets

The Law on the Transformation of Enterprises gave the impetus for the establishment of a bond and more recently a stock market in Hungary. As parent companies sold bonds and stock to banks and foreign investors, an informal market developed, primarily through private placement. This evolved into a nascent bond market which began operation as a weekly meeting at which primarily representatives of banks gathered to sell bonds. This bond market, in turn has become the Budapest Securities Exchange. This Exchange has now been expanded to include stocks as well.

Under the expectation that the stock market will become of increasing importance in Hungary, in 1990 the government passed a law on securities trading which protects securities buyers against fraud. In addition, the Budapest Securities Exchange has introduced a set of rules on capital adequacy and disclosure to provide a second tier of defence[16]. Hungary is now unique in central and eastern Europe in possessing a set of institutions and rules needed for a full-fledged financial system.

The state property agency

The Law on the State Assets Fund and the Administration and Utilisation of its Assets was passed at the same time as the Law on Safeguarding State Assets. The law established an agency to oversee privatisation, the State Property Agency. The Agency is the owner of state-owned property and is responsible for ensuring its appropriate use. It does not carry out sales directly but subcontracts parts of the process through open bidding to companies which are qualified to appraise, sell or consummate sales. It establishes professional control over the process and representation of the state as an owner[17]. The Agency was to begin operation in summer or fall 1990. It will seek professional assistance from foreign banks and state property trust agencies in the West[18].

Other institutions

Hungary also possesses a series of other, unique institutions designed to facilitate its transformation to a market economy. With the passage of the Bankruptcy Law in 1986, the Hungarian Government set up an organisation to facilitate the reorganisation of bankrupt enterprises. The organisation focuses on firms it deems salvageable and attempts to draw in commercial banks early in the process. Once bankruptcy proceedings are initiated, the organisation must decide within 48 hours whether the company is worth saving. This organisation has had a number of applications in 1990 even though its funds have been reduced[19]. If an enterprise looks like it may be saved, the organisation eventually hopes to sell it to the private sector. Thus, it will provide a steady, if small stream of enterprises for privatisation in the coming years.

The Hungarian Government has also set up a Enterprise Development Foundation designed to encourage private enterprise. The Foundation provides money through small banks to private businesses, builds industrial parks, helps generate new financial institutions to support private business, and provides advice and lessons on how to operate private businesses, even though it does not directly invest in them. Through these activities it helps individuals who purchase retail outlets or small state-owned workshops to establish themselves as private entrepreneurs.

Potential policies

Despite the existence of a legal and institutional framework on privatisation and a political consensus that the bulk of state property needs to be privatised, bitter political and policy fights have already begun concerning the form, pace and extent of privatisation. The roots of most of these debates can be found in the various interpretations of the rationales for privatisation.

The process of privatisation

To this point sales of large enterprises have proceeded through the creation of limited liability, joint stock companies. Shares of stock have then often been privately placed through investment banks. Buyers have been Hungarian financial institutions, Western companies or private investors and other Hungarian enterprises. Companies have also sold shares to their own employees. However, widespread issues of shares to the general public have only just begun, primarily because of the previous absence of a stock market.

As shown by the creation of the National Property Agency, a political consensus has emerged demanding that large state enterprises be sold so as to try to obtain "fair" value. Property is to be appraised by an outside appraiser, outside agents are to be hired to advertise for potential buyers and sales are to be conducted openly through various types of auctions or other systems of competitive bidding.

Although Hungarian political leaders concur that this procedure is acceptable for sales of large companies, there are a substantial number of small manufacturing plants, workshops, wholesale and retail outlets that will not be sold as joint stock companies and where the current tenants or employees already possess quasi-property rights which would be politically difficult to dislodge. Many of these organisation have been subject to "spontaneous" privatisation. The director, usually with the support of the workers' council or the assembly of workers, transforms the enterprises into a limited liability company with ownership held by the old enterprise. The new company is then sold (in many cases transferred) to the workforce and the director. In the case of stores, the outlet itself is not privatised, but the manager is able to arrange for a long term lease, sometimes after competitive bidding. State-owned housing has generally been offered for sale to the current tenants.

Public outrage has not focused on these types of privatisation. First, the size of the assets tend to be small. Second, the local communities often feel these individuals already have quasi-property rights. Finally, the transfer accomplishes the objective of transferring property rights and a concern about the profitability of the enterprise to the new owners.

There is a grudging consensus among Hungary's political parties that many avenues towards privatisation should be used. A number of economists, however, have presented schemes for privatisation that have elicited as much or more debate than the programmes of the political parties.

One of the most hotly debated proposals calls for fostering the development of privately-owned businesses by reverse discrimination: state-owned enterprises should be placed under a variety of operating constraints and taxes that will lead to their demise. Private businesses will be encouraged with a favourable regulatory and tax regime.

Not surprisingly, this proposal has been sharply criticised. Ninety-two per cent of Hungary's industrial capital stock is owned by state enterprises. By consigning state-owned firms to gradual bankruptcy, enterprise managers will have few incentives to use this capital stock more efficiently, yet there will be no means through which it can be transferred to private ownership. The proposal calls for Hungary to write off, in effect, this capital, which would lead to an enormous loss of wealth[20].

An alternative proposal has been to give or sell state-owned property to non-profit institutions, state-owned insurance companies and pension funds. Managers of these institutions would be charged with maximising the value of their investments, thus introducing a proper concern for the management of capital in enterprises. This solution also circumvents the problem of the lack of household financial assets available for the purchase of equity in state-owned enterprises.

Other proposals include the sale of shares of enterprises to current employees. This proposal has been sharply criticised as being inequitable. Employees in successful companies benefit while those in unsuccessful companies do not. Another proposal advocates the formation of large mutual funds which own shares in all state-owned companies. Shares in the mutual funds could then be distributed among the population which would buy, sell or hold them. Neither of these proposals appears likely to be adopted.

Privatisation of land

Privatisation of land is one of the most sensitive issues in Hungary. Land has been divided into two classes: land used for residential, commercial and industrial uses, and agricultural land. A large share of residential real estate holdings remained in private hands even after the massive nationalisation of 1949-50. Many of the remaining state holdings are being sold to current residents. Privatisation will be on a bigger scale in commercial real estate, most of which is owned by the state, state enterprises or municipalities. There are some strong fears that foreign enterprises or individuals will make large purchases of this real estate, driving up prices. Not surprisingly, there are restrictions on foreign ownership.

The most ticklish problem politically for Hungary is the privatisation of agricultural land. Individuals already own 11.5 per cent of agricultural land in the form of household plots and the few remaining private farms. In addition, a substantial share of co-operatively farmed land is owned by individual members of the co-operative. Although this land must be farmed jointly, it belongs to the individuals, not to the co-operative as a whole. Full ownership rights to this land have now been restored to the owners. However, if much of this land is no longer farmed by the co-operative, Hungarian agriculture will be plagued by a serious mismatch between the stock of agricultural equipment (large tractors and combines designed for large fields) and the small size of the new farms.

A more serious problem is the privatisation of collectively-owned and state-owned land. One of the coalition partners in the new government the Smallholders Party, ran on the sole policy platform of restoring all property, especially agricultural land, to the owners as of 1947 (after the post World War II land reform). The ensuing costs of identifying the former owners and of the resulting litigation are mind-boggling. Additionally, many of the state farms were previously owned by the Catholic Church or aristocrats. It is difficult to imagine a Hungarian Government restoring all these lands to these groups.

The alternatives to restoration of past property rights include land sales through auctions, transfers and sales to current users, or continued collective ownership, either through the local village or through current members of the collective.

The pace of privatisation

The speed with which enterprises are to be privatised was a major issue in the election campaign. The Free Democrats, the leading opposition party, argues for rapid privatisation citing the arguments that only private owners will use the capital stock efficiently, that the state is incapable of imposing a hard budget constraint on state-owned enterprises, and that enterprise managers are "mining" the capital stock of the country during the current period of uncertainty. Enterprises need to be privatised as quickly as possible so as to stop this behaviour.

The ruling coalition has argued for a slower pace of reform so as to ensure asset sales generate the best possible price, because of the limited financial assets that Hungarians can use to purchase assets, and in order to forestall fraud.

Extent of privatisation and foreign ownership

The Hungarian Democratic Forum, the dominant party, has emphasized obtaining "fair" value for assets. It has also argued for more restrictions on foreign ownership than the largest opposition party or even the pre-election government. The current government has also been more receptive to continued state control of industries they consider key such as banking and telecommunications.

These initial proposals concerning privatisation on the part of the Forum were vague. As late as October 1989 it argued for a socialist economy with mixed forms of ownership. The party programme argued that a "strict market-based economy would only enrich a narrow group and impoverish the majority"[21]. The Forum's attitude toward private property reflected the intellectual legacy of the Revolution of 1956. It has also been supportive of economic democracy in which workers, employers and entrepreneurs would determine economic policy through trade groups, workers' councils and clubs. The October 1989 congress advocated the creation of a democratic society with a competitive, but socially-aware market economy. In sum, the Forum has a strong corporatist slant.

The Forum has argued for dismantling the state sector in a socially controlled and economically rational way. They wish to create a wide stratum of entrepreneurs. However, entrepreneurs would purchase state-owned enterprises as groups, not as individuals. Privatisation would be programmemed; uncontrolled privatisation would discriminate against domestic investors because the limited savings of Hungarians could not compete against foreign capital. They note that total domestic savings of cash and securities equaled 312 billion forints in December 1988 while state enterprises were valued at 2 000 billion forints[22].

This programme creates a number of difficulties, because to this point large scale privatisation has been synonymous with foreign capital. Except for a few directors, the public has had few opportunities to purchase shares of stock.

The programme of the Free Democrats, on the contrary, states that the private sector, despite persecution, is the only successful branch of Hungary's economy. They encourage entrepreneurship and privatisation. They have made the establishment of new private enterprises and the strengthening of existing private enterprises the centre-piece of their economic policy because they believe changing proprietary conditions is the key to transforming the economic structure of the state. They argue for rapid privatisation, but under transparent competitive conditions. They also emphasize that the competitive disadvantages facing small firms should be liquidated. They also argue for making amends to those whose property was expropriated after the Communist take-over through symbolic financial reparations. This would provide moral satisfaction to these people and would signal investors, domestic and foreign, that Hungary guarantees security of investments[23].

One of the most vehement critics of the Free Democrats' programme is the director of the formerly Communist Party trade union. He says, "A few individuals want to resolve all the conflicts and bankruptcy situations that have accumulated to date for their own benefit and to the detriment of the majority... What reason could there be for the series of actions which result in the enrichment of a narrow stratum and the subsequent payment of the bill by the large majority..." [24]. The trade unions have argued for continued state ownership of a large share of state-owned industry and for guaranteed employment.

The previous socialist government also argued for limitations on the extent of privatisation. For example, former Deputy Finance Minister Zsigmond Jarai argued against privatisation of hospitals, schools, oil and gas exploration, and limits on foreign ownership of the press and the banking system[25].

Economic consequences

It is still impossible to systematically evaluate the effects of privatisation using published Hungarian statistics. This is partially due to the short period of time since the initiation of privatisation; privatisation only began in earnest in 1989. Consequently, little data is available concerning its effects. However, a more fundamental problem presents itself. As in the rest of central and eastern Europe, the Hungarian statistical system is designed to collect information from state-owned enterprises. As the state sector diminishes and the private sector grows, a diminishing share of global output will be captured by the traditional, primary statistical indicators. In fact,

Kornai argues that roughly one third of Hungarian GDP was not captured by the statistical office by the mid-1980s, primarily because of tax evasion in the private sector. Below I attempt to assess the initial effects of privatisation using information from the Hungarian press.

The impact of foreign investment

By far and away the most detailed information on privatisation concerns foreign investment. By June 1989 the value of foreign investment in Hungary was 50 billion forints ($833 000 000)[26]. However, most of the shares issued were not listed on the stock market, but had been sold through private placements. It is unclear how much of this capital came in the form of donations in kind (patents, equipment, etc.) and how much in payments to the state. To this point there appears to have been little opposition to foreign investors at the plant or enterprise level. In many cases enterprises have actually sought foreign investors despite the latent threats of layoffs and management turnover. Foreign investors are a source of funds to stave off bankruptcy or pick up the pieces of a bankrupt firm. For example, Translet, a British company, purchased a majority share in an enterprise created from the bankrupt Ganz MAVAG factory for £12 million. Ganz MAVAG had a history of financial problems.

By engaging in a joint venture, the Mecsek Ore Mining Enterprise (MEV), a uranium mining concern, was able to stop liquidation procedures. However, MEV will still have to layoff workers. The capital infusion will allow them to become profitable, by developing a number of sideline activities.

As the Hungarian economy is opened up to import competition, other enterprises are seeking partners that can provide new technologies and products. For example, two small meter producers have been sold to Schlumberger Industries of France. On their own the two producers would probably have had difficulty in competing on the world market. Within Schlumberger they have access to the French firm's technologies and marketing network. Schlumberger receives two operating enterprises with well-trained workforces and a network of clients in central and eastern Europe. It was also motivated by the possibility that its two major competitors, Siemens and General Electric, might purchase the firms, thereby establishing a dominant position in the Hungarian market. After the purchase Schlumberger brought in its own French managers, although it gave the former management a no-layoff guarantee for a few months. The French managers were highly critical of the former Hungarian managers. They argued that they were too bureaucratic and took a very long time to reach decisions.

It is too early to determine the microeconomic effects of foreign shareholders. However, a few examples are instructive. In the case of Schlumberger, the administration is to be dramatically reduced and the workforce cut as well. On the other hand, wages, especially for people on the factory floor, will rise appreciably.

Another major investment was the purchase of half of Tungsram, a large, well-known lighting firm, by an Austrian investment bank in April 1989, which was then resold to General Electric. After large losses in the mid-1980s, Tungsram had been recapitalized by the Budapest Bank in late 1988 which accepted stock as payment on a large, previous loan. It was this stock which was eventually purchased by General Electric.

The new management at Tungsram has claimed to have made substantial improvements in efficiency. According to the new managing director, Gyorgy Varga, the company achieved its highest level of profits in its history in 1989, 1.4 billion forints, seven times the level of 1988. The number of employees fell by 800 and productivity increased 28.6 per cent. Exports to convertible currency areas increased by 30 per cent. The Chairman of the Board, Andras Gabor, ascribed these results to the change in ownership; it enabled the corporation to reduce borrowings and interest expenses as well as restructure.

In the future the management expects to reduce employment further. Varga notes that GE employs 20 000 people world-wide in its lighting source branch and has sales of $2.2 billion. Tungsram has 18 000 employees and sales of $300 million. General Electric plans to invest $50 million in Tungsram by 1994. Varga argued that the amount was limited because the corporation was technically incapable of utilising larger amounts[27].

Foreign investment may turn out to be a disappointing avenue for privatisation. The Hungarian authorities have hoped for capital inflows of $2.5-3 billion annually. As noted above, actual inflows in 1989 were appreciably smaller. Furthermore, many of the Western investments have been in businesses serving the domestic market, especially in services or consumer goods. Western firms in these markets include McDonalds, Citibank, Computerworld, Fotex, Levi Strauss, McCann-Erickson, and Schwinn. Although this is not surprising, many firms on the domestic market earn large rents because of the lack of competition and strictures on imports. The government had hoped that most ventures would be geared toward Western export markets[28].

In short, privatisation involving Western capital appears to have improved the profitability of some Hungarian enterprises. Labour productivity also appears to have improved as many investors have been able to raise wages as well as increase profits. However, some of the investments appear to be geared toward expropriating rents made possible by barriers to imports and are more focused on the domestic market than exports.

Privatisation and Hungarian investors

There has been appreciably less coverage of privatisations involving solely Hungarian investors. Some have argued that managers become more market oriented after privatisation[29]. To this point all conversions of enterprises to privately owned stock companies, joint ventures or limited liability companies have been at the initiative of the former state enterprise managers. They, of course, would be the ones to lose their positions if privatisation proceeded without their participation. Government officials, although they have expressed their intention to arrange for the privatisation of state-owned enterprises, have had neither the energy nor the motivation to implement changes. Because managers have generally initiated privatisation, there has been less turnover in management positions than one might have expected. Most former managers have retained their positions and taken a share of the new firm, thus preserving their positions[30].

There is less anecdotal information on improvements in productivity due to purchases of state-owned enterprises by Hungarians. In contrast to foreign investors,

Hungarians often do not have the marketing expertise or technologies to dramatically improve the position of the firm. However, a few success stories, most notably the buyout of an old steel mill in Ozd, a ferrous metal centre, indicate that significant improvements are possible. However, these improvements have yet to show up in faster rates of growth. Much of the recent increases in Hungarian hard currency exports have come from private or privatised firms. In 1989 of 3 100 enterprises that exported, 600 were private. In 1987 virtually none did so.

Problems of privatisation

Fraud

By far and away the greatest political problem with privatisation is fraud. Hungarian citizens quite naturally become incensed when enterprise managers, many of whom poorly managed their enterprises in the past, are able to profit from their position by selling an enterprise to themselves or to their cronies. As more and more examples have emerged, there has been a political backlash in Hungary that resulted in the law establishing the State Property Agency and close monitoring of state asset sales.

A major scandal revolved around a dummy corporation, the Quintus Company, set up in Sweden to buy HungarHotels, the owner of most of Hungary's finest hotels and restaurants. The investors included some foreigners, but the deal was managed by HungarHotels' management. Quintus paid a small fraction of the value of the hotels. A legal challenge was mounted to abrogate the articles of incorporation because of apparent fraud. Because Hungary lacked the appropriate statutes, incorporation could not be blocked on this basis. The case went to the Hungarian Supreme Court where the contract was declared void on the basis of a technicality.

The directors of HungarHotels would have profited immensely from the deal. They argued that the hotels needed a capital injection for further development and received the backing of the enterprise council. They failed to explain why they had not sought an independent appraisal of the property, why they had not sought open bids from a variety of potential buyers and why the sale needed to be completed in a matter of a few weeks. In fact, they excluded a number of buyers from bidding[31].

What is fascinating about this escapade was how little control the state exercised on privatisation before the passage of the Law on the Protection of State Property. Enterprise managers quite rightly understood that transactions needed to be concluded very quickly because the new law would put an end to the spontaneous privatisation of large enterprises. It is also surprising that managers believed they would be able to get away with something like this.

More recently, Hungarian individuals have been exposed to illicit investment schemes that have led to large-scale losses. A fraudster attracted 100 million forints from private savings for investment in Radius Hungvaricus, a shell company.

Tax collection

Although fraud is an important political problem and may have an appreciable effect on the distribution of wealth and income, its economic effects are probably of lesser importance. Even, if fraudulently acquired, the management of the privatised firm should have a stronger incentive to cut costs and increase profits than would a state-owned firm. Other aspects of privatisation may create more economic problems for Hungarian macroeconomic policy-makers.

Until 1988 the bulk of Hungarian taxes were collected from enterprises either in the form of profit taxes or taxes on factors (capital and labour) through charges on the capital stock and on their wage bill. Profits taxes varied according to the purpose to which they were to be used. Funds going into the reserve fund (savings) were taxed at much lower rates than funds placed in the development fund (investment) or funds for increasing wages. Other major sources of revenue were social security taxes, turnover taxes (product-specific sales taxes) and tariffs.

In 1988 taxes on capital were abolished and taxes on profits reduced. As the private sector and second jobs expanded, the state wanted to tax these additional incomes in order to mitigate disparities in incomes. By replacing business taxes with an income tax and VAT, the state was able to impose a greater share of the tax burden on individuals with multiple incomes or who have higher than average levels of consumption.

The Hungarian Government still depends on the state enterprise sector to collect much of its taxes. In the past the state has had many of the same problems the Italian Government has had in collecting taxes from the private sector. Enterprises keep two sets of books, many transactions are conducted in cash and many entrepreneurs do not bother to register with the state. Although the imposition of income taxes and VAT has served to create the structure for a modern tax system, the Hungarian Government may experience some precipitous declines in revenue as more enterprises move from the state sector to private hands, unless it can ensure the administrative and enforcement apparatus for collecting taxes from this sector are functioning well.

Unemployment and the reallocation of labour

The major popular worry about privatisation is large scale layoffs of Hungarian workers. As noted above, foreign companies that have purchased Hungarian firms have invariably reduced the workforce, especially the administrative staff. Hungarians are cognizant that most factories and offices are overmanned by Western standards and that widescale privatisation will result in layoffs.

Overmanning is the result of the Hungarian Government's policy of full employment adopted in the late 1940s. This was defined as assuring each worker that he may retain his current job as long as he wishes. Despite high rates of labour turnover in many industries, layoffs were almost unheard of. This policy was implemented by generating permanent excess demand for labour by keeping the relative price of labour low through incomes policies and through ministerial pressure not to allow layoffs. The converse of this was ministerial acceptance of poor profitability performance, if the enterprises argued that it was an important employer. For example, Ganz-Mavag, a locomotive producer, the steel works at Ozd, and the Csepel Trust, located in the working class district to the south of Budapest, have had long histories of endemic losses which were covered in order to forestall layoffs.

Government policy-makers in the new government are carefully taking into consideration the consequences of rapid privatisation for employment. They believe it will be easier to pressure enterprises to retain workers if they still belong to the state.

It will also be easier politically to provide employment subsidies to state-owned enterprises than to enterprises that have recently been sold to the private sector. For these reasons, the new Hungarian Government may be unlikely to accelerate privatisation and may even slow it.

Hungarian businesses are likely to be heavily taxed to pay for large subsidies, if the government attempts to preserve many jobs in the state sector. These taxes are likely to slow capital formation, the creation of small businesses, and the transformation of Hungary into a market economy. As shown by the ease with which foreign investors can reduce their workforces without affecting output, as well as the poor quality of many Hungarian services, Hungary still needs to transfer labour from administration and manufacturing into services. This process will be slowed, if taxes impede the formation and growth of new businesses. Thus, if the new government focuses on preserving current jobs, Hungary will be in for a longer, more costly period of transition.

Legal costs

Hungary is already suffering from a spate of law suits over ownership brought by the former owners of a number of enterprises and buildings. To this point the Hungarian Supreme Court has discouraged litigation by noting that the losers of the suit would be responsible for court costs and legal fees of the other party[32]. However, if litigation becomes commonplace it will slow the process of privatisation and induce a great deal of uncertainty into the process of investing in the Hungarian economy, thereby slowing the transformation of the economy.

Conclusions

Privatisation, at least when it involves foreign investors, appears to produce many of the improvements in enterprise performance that its supporters claim. Profits and wages are increased, indicating improvements in labour and capital productivity. New technologies are introduced and hard currency exports have risen in some cases. On the other hand, employment has been reduced and in many cases managers argue that further cuts are inevitable. Some of the same phenomena, although not as well documented, have occurred in privatisations involving Hungarians only.

Privatisation promises many problems as well. Fraud has been the most politically visible. With the passage of the Law on the Protection of State Property fraud should diminish, at the cost, however, of a slower pace of privatisation. Fraud may lead to a political backlash, but to this point pressure has been exerted to make the privatisation more transparent rather than halt it altogether. A second problem may be increased difficulty in collecting taxes, as a greater share of total output is produced by small, private firms. If tax evasion is on a large enough scale, the Hungarian Government could have severe fiscal problems with the resulting macroeconomic consequences.

Fears of unemployment could slow the pace of privatisation as well as the process of restructuring. The costs of this policy may not be readily apparent, but would show up in slower rates of capital formation and economic growth. An additional problem may be widespread litigation over property rights on the part of past owners. If this becomes a widely used avenue to obtain property, the privatisation programme would be severely retarded, foreign investment discouraged and the transition period greatly extended.

Notes

1. Halmai (1987), p. 57.
2. The largest 100 enterprises in Hungary account for the bulk of state-owned assets in industry.
3. *Heti Vilaggazdasag* (1986), 18 October, p. 50.
4. *Heti Vilaggazdasag* (1987).
5. Laki (1984).
6. Crane (1983), Gacs (1980).
7. Tardos (1990), *Nepszabadsag.*
8. Ward (1967), Chapter 8.
9. Tardos (1990), *Nepszabadsag; Figyelo* (1990).
10. Merth (1989).
11. *Heti Vilaggazdasag* (1988).
12. *Magyar Hirlap* (1990).
13. Tompe (1990).
14. *Heti Vilaggazdasag* (1990), "Hagyatekgondozas".
15. *Heti Vilaggazdasag* (1990), "Listing Stocks: Baring the Figures".
16. Tompe (1990).
17. Kocsis (1990).
18. *Figyelo* (1990), "Bankruptcy Liquidation".
19. Tardos (1990), *Nepszabadsag*, 3 January.
20. Radio Free Europe (1989), "The Democratic Forum's Economic programme".
21. Radio Free Europe (1989), "The Democratic Forum's Economic programme."
22. *Heti Vilaggazdasag* (1990), "ZDSz: programme to Encourage Entrepreneurship".
23. *Nepszava* (1990).
24. Kocsis (1990).
25. Radio Free Europe (1989), "The First Experiences of Privatisation".
26. Egerszegi (1990).
27. Magas (1990).
28. Magas (1990).
29. Radio Free Europe (1989), "The First Experiences of Privatisation".
30. Gal (1990).
31. Fahidi (1990).

References

ADAM, J. (1987), "The Hungarian Economic Reform of the 1980s", *Soviet Studies,* Vol. 39, No. 4, October.

CRANE (1983).

CSIKOS-NAGY, B. (1982), *Gazdasagpolitika,* Kossuth Publishing House, Budapest.

EGERSZEGI, C. (1990), "After Successful Change of Ownership: Millions of Dollars for Tungram", *Nepszabadsag,* 1 March, p. 6.

FAHIDI, G. (1990), "Reprivatizalasi Kerdojelek," *Heti Vilaggazdasag,* 21 April, p. 69.

FIGYELO (1990), "Bankruptcy Liquidation," 4 Januar 1990, p. 6.

FINK, G. (1982), "Determinants of Sectoral Investment Allocation in Hungary," *Acta Oeconomica,* Vol. 28, No. 3-4, pp. 375-388.

GACS, J. (1980), *Importkorlatok, hianyjelensegek es a vallalat alkalmazkodas, Konjunktura es Piackutato Intezet,* Budapest.

GACS, J. (1987), "Import Substitution and Investments in Hungary in the Period of Restrictions (1979-86)", in *Investment System and Foreign Trade Implications in Hungary,* Andras Raba and Karl-Ernst Schenk, eds., Gustav Fischer Verlag, Stuttgart.

GAL, Z. (1990), "What is Yours is Mine," *Nepszabadsag,* 13 January, p. 8.

GEY, P., J. Kosta and W. Quaisser (1987), *Crisis and Reform in Socialist Economies,* Westview, Boulder, Colorado.

HALMAI, G. (1987), "The Investment Decision-Making System and its Legal Regulation," in *Investment System and Foreign Trade Implications in Hungary,* Andras Raba and Karl-Ernst Schenk, eds., Gustav Fischer Verlag, Stuttgart.

HETI VILAGGAZDASAG (1986), "Nyeresegerdekteleneseg", 18 October, 1986, p. 50.

HETI VILAGGAZDASAG (1987), "HVG Interju: Valazszol egy vallalatvezeto", Vol. 9, No. 45, 7 November, p. 62.

HETI VILAGGAZDASAG (1988), "Mutoasztalon," 16 April, pp. 50-52.

HETI VILAGGAZDASAG (1990) "Hagyatekgondozas," Vol. 9, No. 50, p. 52.

HETI VILAGGAZDASAG (1990), "Listing Stocks: Baring the Figures", 13 February, p. 76.

HETI VILAGGAZDASAG (1990), "ZDSz: programme to Encourage Entrepreneurship", 20 January, p. 8.

KOCSIS, G. (1990), "Everything's for Sale?", *Heti Vilaggazdasag,* 20 January, p. 15.

KORNAI, J. (1980), *The Economics of Shortage,* North-Holland, New York.

KORNAI, J. (1986), "The Hungarian Reform Process: Visions, Hopes, and Reality", *Journal of Economic Literature,* Vol. 24, No. 4, December, pp. 1687-1737.

KOSTA, J. (1988), "Economic Policy in Soviet-Type Economies: Overview and Outline for Further Discussion", in *The Economies of Eastern Europe Under Gorbachev's Influence,* Colloquium 1988, NATO-Economics Directorate, Brussels, March.

LAKI, M. (1984), "The Enterprise Crisis," *Acta Oeconomica,* Vol. 32, No. 1-2, 1984, pp. 113-124.

MAGAS, I. (1990), "Reforms Under Pressure: Hungary", *East European Quarterly,* Spring, p. 93.

MAGYAR HIRLAP (1990), "Draft Law on State Assets Fund," 8 January, pp. 8-10.

MAKO, C. (1987), "Enterprise Councils: Tools of Management or Tools of Workers?", March, mimeo.

MARER, P. (1986), "Economic Reform in Hungary: From Central Planning to Regulated Market," in *Joint Economic Committee of Congress, East European Economies: Slow Growth in the 1980s,* U.S. Government Printing Office, Washington D.C., pp. 223-297.

MERTH, L. (1989), "Abuse of privatisation Analyzed," *Heti Vilaggazdasag,* 23 December, pp. 65-67.

NEPSZAVA (1990), "Open letter from SZOT President Sandor Nagy to Prime Minister Miklos Nemeth," 6 January, p. 3.

RABA, A. and K.E. Schenk, eds. (1987), *Investment System and Foreign Trade Implications in Hungary,* Gustav Fischer Verlag, Stuttgart.

Radio Free Europe (1989), "The Democratic Forum's Economic programme", Hungarian Situation Report/17, 30 November, p. 23.

Radio Free Europe (1989), "The First Experiences of Privatisation," Hungarian Situation Report/17, 30 November, p. 27.

SOOS, K.A. (1986), "Informal Pressures, Mobilization and Campaigns in Centrally Planned Economies", *EUI Working Paper* No. 86/246, European University Institute, Florence.

TARDOS, M. (1990), "From a People's Republic to a Republic: The Operation is More Painful than Kornai Thinks," *Nepszabadsag,* 3 January, p. 8.

TARDOS, M. (1990), "CMEA Market Change; Fund Without Money," *Figyelo,* 15 February, p. 7.

TOMPE, I. (1990), "Passionate Thoughts on Property and Managers Interests", *Nepszabadsag,* 9 January, p. 8.

WARD (1967), Chapter 8.

Strategies for Economic Transformation in Central and Eastern Europe: Role of Financial Market Reform

Lawrence J. Brainard

Introduction

What role should the reform of financial markets play in the economic transformation of central and eastern European countries into market economic systems? Two perspectives are essential in addressing this question: 1) What is the fundamental goal of the transformation process and how does financial market reform contribute to achieving that goal? 2) Where are we today in the reform process and what near-term changes in financial markets are necessary in order to move toward that goal?

Where economic transformation should lead

It may be commonplace to remark that economic growth is the goal of the transformation process, but many seem to forget that market reforms of these economies are not an end in themselves. The challenge is to create economic systems in central and eastern Europe that will generate self-sustaining economic growth under conditions of stable prices. Growth is central to the political legitimacy of the reform efforts; a failure to boost growth, and with it personal incomes, would seriously undermine popular support for the new democratic regimes. Furthermore, growth should be the yardstick against which alternative adjustment strategies are evaluated. Any viable adjustment strategy must go beyond economic stabilization efforts to spell out a feasible process that leads to the revival of growth and investment in these economies.

The creation of a real market for capital, where resources are allocated efficiently, is an essential component of the economic transformation. The pay-off from stabilization and economic reform will not be forthcoming unless capital is allocated efficiently. The most important institutional element of the capital market is the banking system. Markets for equities and government bonds could play an increasingly important role in the development of capital markets in central and eastern Europe, but in the near- and medium-term, the bulk of savings will flow

The original draft of this study was awarded First Prize in The 1990 AMEX Bank Review Awards. The author is indebted to Professor *Michael Marrese* and the Centre for the Co-operation with European Economies in Transition for their encouragement of my research.

95

through the banking system. The issue of banking system reform, therefore, is central to efforts to improve the efficiency of resource use.

A second requirement for ensuring efficient allocation of resources is that the users of investment capital should be responsible for its effective application. This implies the privatisation of ownership of much of the capital in these countries, and effective disciplines on those firms remaining under state management. In other words, privatisation, improved financial discipline and banking reform are related aspects of the same resource efficiency goal.

Enterprise restructuring, privatisation and banking reform must go forward together. Privatisation without banking reform would fail to ensure that capital is allocated to the firms that can use the resources most effectively. This will only hamper the hoped-for supply-side response essential for increased economic growth. Furthermore, firms will not face effective financial disciplines until the banking system can refuse to provide additional credit to given borrowers, i.e. banks must be able to enforce the "hard budget" constraint. A banking reform without enterprise restructuring and privatisation, in turn, would only perpetuate the accumulation of bad loans in the portfolios of the banks.

The success of privatisation and financial disciplines for state firms, therefore, is tied to the creation of banks that are capable of exercising independent credit judgements. This is not going to happen unless banks are forced to protect their own capital position against credit losses. Banks cannot defend their own capital until their existing balance sheets are cleaned up to identify what those capital positions are. Banking reform, therefore, should focus on the restructuring of the existing commercial banks to achieve this end.

This point is also relevant to western efforts to increase flows of new credits to support reform efforts in central and eastern Europe. Unless the existing banks are restructured, the new western resources going into the country will likely be misused, thus perpetuating the power of the nomenklatura and the influence of the existing economic structure over resource allocation.

A second goal of banking reform is to create the institutional framework for effective control of the money supply by the central bank. This is more than a technical question of reserve requirements or instruments for open-market operations. One essential change is to free the banks – both the central bank and the commercial banks – from their traditional roles as financiers of the fiscal deficit and of the losses of the state-owned enterprises. This change is closely related to the reforms discussed in the preceding paragraph.

A further aspect of monetary control involves bringing central and eastern Europe's burgeoning informal credit markets under effective supervision. Inter-enterprise credit markets have emerged in recent years in response to central bank efforts to tighten credit conditions. Such disintermediation of credit flows is a major factor acting to weaken the effectiveness of monetary policy.

Where does the reform effort stand today?

Many reform efforts have been launched in central and eastern Europe over the past decade; most have failed. A relevant question, therefore, is why effective reform has been so hard to achieve.

The economic structures of central and eastern European countries are seriously distorted, giving rise to the wastage of economic resources on a massive scale. Some of these resource losses are easily identified, for example, irrational relative prices and budget subsidies to loss-making enterprises. The sensible policy in this case is economic stabilization, such as balancing the budget, freeing prices and increasing competitive forces in the economy.

If economic stabilization were the only concern, the task of economic transformation would at least be clearly outlined, even if still hard to achieve. But the evidence suggests otherwise. Economic stabilization efforts over the past decade in Yugoslavia, Poland and Hungary have not led to a recovery of economic growth, in part because these efforts so far have not successfully dealt with serious economic imbalances embedded in the structure of these economic systems. In order to address these problems, countries must move beyond conventional stabilization programs to implement comprehensive structural reforms.

Serious structural imbalances in these countries today are lodged in their banks, which have been the repository of decades of accumulated losses of state-owned firms. Socialist banks are engaged in a misallocation of resources of massive proportions, and most of these losses do not find reflection in conventional measures of the government's fiscal deficit.

Some data will serve to highlight the dimensions of the problem. In 1987 in Yugoslavia, for example, the government's fiscal accounts showed a small surplus, but losses recorded by the National Bank of Yugoslavia (NBY) amounted to a staggering 8.5 per cent of GDP. The NBY losses resulted from the redistribution of resources to loss-making enterprises through the banking system by means of negative real rates of interest on outstanding loans[1]. In Poland, the World Bank estimated that interest rate subsidies provided to state enterprises through the banking system totalled 10 per cent of GDP in 1988[2].

Another less-than-evident source of such resource losses through the banking system derives from the massive portfolio of bad loans held by commercial banks in central and eastern European countries. Faced by the refusal and inability of loss-making enterprises to service existing credits, the banks have simply refinanced such loans and provided new ones on top of the old ones in order to pay the interest. Neither the banks nor the government have been willing to push companies into bankruptcy.

In Yugoslavia, for example, the National Bank estimates that troubled loans account for over 40 per cent of the loan portfolio of the commercial banks, with potential losses totalling as much as 25 per cent of loans ($7-9 billion), far in excess of the banks' capital[3]. Accurate data on bad loans in other countries is unavailable, but potential losses are undoubtedly of similar magnitude.

Questionable accounting and supervisory practices have also helped obscure these hidden losses. In Hungary, for example, the three major commercial banks inherited a substantial portfolio of troubled loans when they were set up by the

97

l Bank in 1987. These banks have capitalised interest payments due and ￼ interest as income on non-performing loans, with the result that the banks' ￼ed income statements depart substantially from generally accepted accounting proc...ures (GAAP) in the West. Although the banks have consistently reported profitable operations, their loan portfolios have, until recently, not been audited for collectibility and reserve funds for doubtful loans are inadequate[4].

Stabilization and structural reform – the Polish model

Experience with failed reform programs in central and eastern Europe since 1980 suggests that economic stabilization and structural reform are both essential components of a viable economic transformation strategy. The key issue is the sequencing of stabilization and structural reforms. Should stabilization efforts move forward, while the ground is being prepared for structural reforms? Or do stabilization and structural reform need to be synchronised in some way? A discussion of the recent Polish economic shock program will serve to highlight the dimensions of the sequencing issue.

The Polish economic program introduced on 1 January 1990 is predicated on decisive and rapid change in economic policy. The initial policy shock is focused on economic stabilization measures such as:

    i)   a balanced fiscal budget, tight credit ceilings and controls on wage-setting in state enterprises;

    ii) the freeing of most prices to find their market-clearing levels;

    iii) removal of bureaucratic restrictions on the private sector;

    iv) increased competition by means of a sharp devaluation followed by the pegging of the zloty at a competitive rate.

The Polish Program anticipated a phased introduction of structural changes, though the importance of a rapid introduction of such changes is clearly recognised. Jeffrey Sachs, who advised the Poles responsible for drawing up the program, explained that "...Poland's goal is to establish the economic, legal, and institutional basis for a private-sector market economy in just one year"[5]. The introduction of comprehensive stabilization measures was not held up pending the introduction of structural reforms. The basic Polish strategy, therefore, was rapid and severe economic stabilization, followed by a phased introduction of structural changes.

In assessing the Polish Program, several issues deserve emphasis. One is that stabilization measures imply a severe, immediate reduction of real incomes, but without a clear identification of where or how the hoped-for supply response is to be achieved. There are certainly efficiencies to be gained through the creation of unregulated markets, but most potential market participants lack the resources to respond to the opportunities such unfettered markets offer. The hoped-for supply response depends primarily on structural reforms of the markets for labour and capital, not on stabilization. The Polish Program has little to say on how factor markets are to be created[6].

The sequencing of the Polish Program – harsh stabilization, followed by phased reform – also introduced a volatile element of political instability into the reform effort. Workers are unlikely to accept substantial reductions in real incomes without going on strike, unless tangible benefits of their sacrifices become evident in fairly short order. In the early months of the shock program the average Polish standard of living declined substantially in real terms – over 30 per cent, but strikes were rather limited.

With the passage of time, however, the policy makers' political vulnerability to workers' protests increases. Unless growth can be revived quickly, workers' opposition to continued austerity puts the structural reforms at risk. But renewed growth depends more on structural reforms, than on stabilization. Thus, the delayed sequencing of such structural reforms in the Polish Program suggests a vulnerability in the overall economic strategy.

The announcement by the Polish Government of an easing of the austerity program in June suggests that Polish leaders are having second thoughts about the viability of the original strategy[7]. The official press release announced that the switch to a free market economy was completed in just five months, but this cannot be seen as credible. None of the critical structural reforms promised in January have been achieved. Indeed, the new law on privatisation, which had been promised by no later than March, was not passed by the Parliament until the end of July; further delays are expected until the new Ministry of Property Transformation – which is to oversee the privatisation – is set up and begins to operate[8].

It is too early to say how political developments will slow down efforts to introduce structural reforms. It does seem, however, that the over-riding, initial emphasis on radical stabilization moves was misplaced. It acted to slow progress on the difficult structural reform measures by focusing the attention of key policy makers elsewhere. The shock program also reflected a naive optimism about the reinvigoration of growth through the free play of market forces, while missing the fact that structural impediments in the markets for labour and capital remained largely untouched.

An initial judgement about shock programs, such as the Polish one, is that it is a mistake to launch a radical economic stabilization until key structural reforms are ready to be implemented. Stabilization efforts are obviously unavoidable in the context of hyperinflation and serious price distortions. Greater priority, however, must be accorded efforts to accelerate the structural reforms and to achieve a closer synchronisation between reform and stabilization.

A second concern about the Polish program is that its agenda of structural reforms seems to overemphasize privatisation. In his lengthy exposition of the Polish model in *The Economist,* Sachs devotes considerable attention to problems of privatisation, but he ignores problems of the banking system and the need to create a real capital market in Poland[9].

There are two key reasons why banking reforms are essential to strategies of economic transformation in central and eastern Europe. One is that privatisation cannot succeed without a functioning capital market. And a capital market cannot be created unless a thorough reform of the banking system is enacted. Privatisation and banking system reform, therefore, must go together.

The second reason is that the banking system is a serious source of economic disequilibrium in all of these countries. As the Yugoslav case cited earlier illustrated, it is possible for the government's fiscal budget to be in balance at the same time that huge unrecognised losses are piling up in the banks.

As detailed in the next section, there are two distinct aspects to banking reform. Banks must not be allowed to continue making bad loans; enterprise restructuring through privatisation and moving loss-making firms into bankruptcy and tighter prudential supervision on the banks' loan portfolios are essential steps here. But reforms must go beyond such measures. For banks to make a positive contribution to the efficient allocation of capital resources, it will be necessary to clean up the banks' balance sheets by writing off troubled loans and by injecting new capital. We turn now to a detailed look at the state of central and eastern European banking systems.

The condition of socialist banking and finance

The traditional banking model in central and eastern Europe consisted of a central bank and several special-purpose banks, one dealing with individuals' savings and other banking needs and the other focused on foreign financial activities. The central bank provided most of the commercial banking needs of enterprises in addition to the usual functions of a central bank.

In recent years, central and eastern European countries have modified this structure by carving all of the commercial banking activities out of the central bank and transferring them to new commercial banks. In most countries the new banks were set up along industry lines, while in Poland the banks were set up on a regional basis. The creation of these new banks is relatively recent:

Country	Date	New State-Owned Banks
Bulgaria	1987	7
Czechoslovakia	1990	2
Eastern Germany	1990	1
Hungary	1987	3
Poland	1988	9

Although a number of small *de novo* banks were also allowed, mainly in Poland and Hungary, the new state-owned commercial banks controlled the bulk of the financial transactions of the enterprise sector[10].

These banks were all created by transferring existing loans from the portfolio of the central bank to the new institutions. The banks, thus, started life with an inherited overhang of troubled assets, in most cases highly concentrated by enterprise and industry. Furthermore, competition was restricted because the banks were not allowed to deal with enterprises other than those assigned to them.

Hobbled with such handicaps, the new banks cannot play a role in any way similar to the role played by sound banking institutions active in western capital markets. They do not have their own capital resources. If their loan assets were marked to realistic values, the banks would show negative net worth. In extending new loans, therefore, the bank is not putting its own capital resources at risk, since any potential losses will accrue in one way or another to the government – either the government must inject new capital from the budget to cover such losses or, more probably, the losses will be covered up by the authorities agreeing with the bank not to recognise such bad loans. The fact that the losses are not recognised implies an

100

accumulation of contingent liabilities on the account of the government's fiscal budget, since the government will have to cover such losses sooner or later out of budgetary resources[11].

The new state-owned commercial banks should be viewed more as fiscal agents of the Treasury, than as banks in their own right. They collect a large part of the government's inflation tax on enterprise cash balances and redistribute resources to enterprises through interest rate subsidies (i.e. negative real rates) and additional loans to cover interest due[12].

Furthermore, the banks have limited leverage over their borrowers. If the firm does not have the money, it simply refuses to pay. The bank is forced to extend a new loan to recognise the non-payment. Unless the government is willing to throw a firm into bankruptcy – so far a rare occurrence – the bank cannot pursue an active credit policy. The existing banking structure, therefore, is acting as a fiscal "black hole", misallocating loan capital to cover the losses of the state-owned enterprises.

A substantial volume of losses is also carried on the balance sheets of the central banks or foreign trade banks of these countries. These losses have resulted from periodic currency devaluations. In most countries the foreign debt is carried as a liability on the central bank's books[13]. Devaluation increases the local currency value of foreign liabilities; to balance this rise in liabilities, an offsetting asset must be entered, usually identified as a "valuation adjustment". In reality, of course, there are no real resources behind such an "asset", since the enterprises have been relieved of any exchange rate risk.

The balance sheet losses from devaluations carried by central banks are staggering. In Hungary, recent estimates put the stock of National Bank losses at about 30 per cent of GDP, or about $7 billion[14]. In Yugoslavia, the valuation losses carried on the consolidated balance sheet of the National Bank are over 60 per cent of total assets[15].

Approaches to financial market reforms

Attempts to improve financial sector performance have been included in all central and eastern European country programs of the IMF and World Bank in recent years. The meagre results from such reform efforts serve to highlight why financial reforms are so difficult to implement.

Starting with Yugoslavia in 1983, financial reform has focused on eliminating financial losses associated with credit flows. The primary policy measures included the introduction of positive real rates of interest on deposits and loans and the tightening of credit conditions by imposing credit ceilings.

The typical result of such tight credit policies was a rapid growth in payment arrears between firms. In the context of relatively monopolised market structures, few firms could afford to cut off an important buyer of a given product, so they tolerated such arrears. In any case, the country's legal systems did not furnish the creditor enterprises strong legal means to force repayment. As a result the practice of financing via inter-enterprise credit spread throughout the economy.

The disintermediation of credit flows through the growth in inter-enterprise credit has now reached significant proportions. In Yugoslavia, the share of inter-enterprise credits in total credit increased from 26 per cent in 1980 to 39 per cent in 1987[16]. In Hungary, the so-called "credit queues" rose dramatically in 1988-89, when the National Bank implemented a tight monetary policy as part of its IMF Standby Agreement. There is reason to believe that the disintermediation of credit flows has increased since the implementation earlier this year of stabilization programs in Poland, Hungary and Yugoslavia.

These developments are worrisome because they act to reduce the effectiveness of restrictive monetary policies on aggregate demand – the growth of inter-enterprise credits has so far escaped such controls. And since such credits are inadequately captured in the credit data, the central bank's ability to gauge the tightness of monetary policy is also hampered. The danger is that monetary policy will appear much more restrictive than it really is.

New perspectives on financial reforms

The stock answer in every proposal to reform central and eastern Europe's financial markets has always been the same – to increase the financial disciplines in the system. Such efforts have so far failed to produce acceptable results because none of these reform efforts has yet addressed the balance sheet losses which lie at the heart of the problem. Banks and governments have been unwilling to push firms into bankruptcy – the banks fear the financial impact on their balance sheets and the governments fear the unemployment consequences. As a result, firms have never had to pay the ultimate price for their misdeeds.

The only effective way to implement financial discipline is to go beyond the current measures, which focus on subsidies and credit flows, to clean up the balance sheets of enterprises and banks. The reform must seek to allocate the unrealised losses on the balance sheets of enterprises and banks. Financial discipline (hard budget constraints) must be translated into balance sheet realities for each firm. The issue for policy makers is how to allocate such losses among the workers, the creditors and the government's budget (i.e. society at large).

For enterprises, the mechanisms for sanitizing balance sheets include bankruptcy, rehabilitation and/or privatisation. Bankruptcy implies losses for the workers – through employment – and the liquidation of financial claims on the enterprise, i.e. losses for the creditors. The rehabilitation of enterprises with reasonable prospects of profitable operation would likely require wage sacrifices from workers and partial debt relief from creditor banks. Privatisation, properly managed and implemented, may be viewed as an alternative way for the state to translate firms' balance sheets to current values, since any sale should ideally yield a cash benefit to the government's fiscal budget equal to the firm's net worth[17].

In practice, the implications for the fiscal budget of any of these options will be significant. The government must pick up the costs of unemployment benefits, it will need to subsidise the losses of the state-owned banks, it will be called upon to inject additional resources into enterprise "workouts", and it will not likely be able to realise cash benefits from privatisations equal to firms' net worth in most cases.

Viewing the issue of financial discipline in such a balance sheet perspective serves to underscore the need for a comprehensive fiscal framework and a set of clear priorities for action as a prerequisite for structural reform. The restructuring will undoubtedly be costly, and the authorities need to monitor costs carefully. Otherwise, the natural tendency to push most of these losses in an unplanned and piecemeal fashion into the fiscal budget will quickly swamp the ability of the government to balance the fiscal accounts, thus reigniting inflationary pressures. This perspective also highlights the urgent need for credible balance sheet valuations, which require the implementation of western accounting principles and practices.

Finally, privatisation may be seen as the logical outcome of a set of comprehensive measures to clean up enterprise balance sheets. Many discussions of privatisations focus exclusively on techniques of privatisation, without adequate attention to the fiscal dimensions of the privatisation process. An important prerequisite of any privatisation strategy is that it be compatible with the government's fiscal control efforts.

Cleaning up the balance sheets of the banks poses a separate set of issues. A thorough restructuring of enterprise balance sheets will contribute much to eliminating bank losses from ongoing credit activities. Restructuring of enterprises and banks should, therefore, proceed together. But the losses in the banks' loan portfolios raise a somewhat different set of problems. There is little social value in pushing any of the state-owned banks into bankruptcy, given their pivotal role in the financial system. The only viable option is to restructure the banks.

The best way to do this is to recapitalise the banks by first lifting the bad loans out of their portfolios and then to provide a mechanism for injecting new capital. One approach used in Chile in the mid-1980s and now being implemented in Yugoslavia is for the government to "purchase" the banks' bad loans (identified by means of a special portfolio audit) with long-term bonds paying a positive interest spread over the banks' cost of funds. The capital of the banks would grow over time, thanks to the elimination of problem loans and the positive net income flow from the government bonds.

Given improved accounting practices and effective prudential supervision, the banks could over time be transformed into profitable institutions, thus forming the core of an emergent capital market structure. The persistent foreign exchange losses of the central banks should be controlled by holding the enterprises accountable for the foreign risk on new external borrowings.

Over time, the government would have to absorb the losses on the bad loans and transfer new resources to the banks via interest payments on the bonds. These actions could prove costly to the fiscal budget, but the costs of inaction may be even higher[18]. An alternative approach would be for the government to assist in spinning off a bank's bad loans into a separate entity, managed by a special work-out team from the bank. This would create a "good" bank and a "bad" bank; special incentives could be provided to the management team to help maximise value from the work-out process. The "good" bank would provide the focus of new capital market activity[19].

Whatever structure is chosen, the important goal is to create viable institutions quickly to provide the impetus for the development of a real capital market. This can only be done if the existing overhang of bad loans is removed from the banks' portfolios.

Strategies for economic transformation – a summing up

It is time to bring together the various elements touched on in this paper that outline a possible strategy for the economic transformation of central and eastern European economies:

i) The revival of economic growth in central and eastern Europe requires the creation of factor markets, especially a market for capital.

ii) Financial market reform is central to efforts to improve the efficiency of resource allocation; successful privatisation requires a functioning capital market.

iii) The introduction of structural reforms should be synchronised as much as possible with major economic stabilization efforts; it is a mistake to undertake radical economic stabilization until key structural reforms are ready to be implemented.

iv) The key structural reforms involve cleaning up the balance sheets of the enterprises and banks; these reforms must go forward together.

v) The unrealised enterprise balance sheet losses should be addressed through bankruptcy, rehabilitation of viable enterprises, and privatisation; the balance sheet losses of the commercial banks should be addressed by means of a recapitalisation of the banks.

vi) The recapitalisation of the commercial banks is an essential step in the creation of a capital market and in the improvement of the effectiveness of monetary policy.

vii) The above-mentioned reforms come with significant fiscal costs; governments should employ a comprehensive fiscal framework and clear priorities to prevent a haemorrhaging of the fiscal accounts.

There is a final, very practical consideration – whether the recasting of the existing banks into modern capital market institutions can be achieved quickly and at an affordable cost to the government budget. The potential contribution that foreign involvement may make to the success of the strategy is relevant in this regard.

A discussion of changes introduced in eastern Germany (German Democractic Republic before the unification of Germany) banking system resulting from monetary union earlier in July 1990 will serve to outline these issues. Although the extensive financial support offered by western Germany (Federal Republic of Germany before the unification of Germany) makes eastern Germany a special case, their efforts to create a functioning capital market virtually overnight have highlighted problems that are relevant to reform efforts in other central and eastern European countries.

The sole, state-owned commercial bank, Kreditbank, was created in April 1990 by the transfer of all commercial accounts from the eastern German central bank, the Staatsbank. In reality, the Kreditbank was nothing more than the former commercial departments of the Staatsbank. Recognising that it possessed little experience or competence in commercial banking under the competitive market conditions that would exist with monetary union, the Kreditbank entered into joint ventures in June with two large western German commercial banks, Deutsche Bank and Dresdner Bank[20].

As its contribution to these joint ventures, Kreditbank put up its branch offices (real estate, furnishings and equipment) and transferred some 13 000 personnel. In effect, all of its branches were spun off into the two joint ventures. But its entire DM 120 billion portfolio of old loans to eastern German enterprises remained with the parent institution, which is now reduced to a shell holding company with only 250 employees[21].

The eastern German banking reform is following a strategy similar to that suggested above of creating a "bad" bank to hold the portfolio of bad enterprise loans and a "good" bank to facilitate the quick startup of a modern, western banking system helped by capital infused by the western partners. Several aspects of this strategy, though, warrant further scrutiny.

The decision to leave all commercial loans in a single entity, rather than just the bad loans, was likely motivated by the political urgency of achieving monetary union as quickly as possible. There was not sufficient time to conduct a portfolio audit to identify good and bad loans nor to explore other options to liquidate the loans via privatisations of enterprises. There was also not a clear definition of what was to happen with the old enterprise loans once they were isolated in the Kreditbank, although it was understood that such decisions would have to be negotiated in Bonn, not in eastern Germany.

This has created a moral hazard problem for the western German authorities. No institutional structure is available to manage the "work-out" of these loans; the new joint venture banks have no direct interest in pressing for the repayment of the loans. There is, thus, a strong incentive for good eastern German enterprises to default on their loans, given a general expectation that western Germany will pick up the tab for the losses on the debt. As financial problems of eastern German enterprises mounted in the wake of monetary union, the western Germany Economics Ministry belatedly proposed a one year freeze on servicing of the corporate debt[22].

At the same time, the lack of enterprise audits according to western GAAP methodology and legal uncertainties associated with land and other security for loans are hindering the new lending operations of the joint venture banks. Accurate balance sheet data on enterprises are lacking to guide lending decisions and the legal uncertainties complicate efforts to use various assets to secure borrowings. Faced with a growing demand for increased federal guarantees on eastern German loans, Chancellor Helmut Kohl took the unusual step in early August of calling in the banks to try to persuade them to step up their lending on their own account[23].

The decision by the eastern German authorities to seek joint ventures with western German banks in order to "jump start" the process of creating a modern banking system involves significant concessions on both sides. Eastern Germany granted a potentially lucrative domestic banking franchise to outside banks, but in return the country will benefit from a substantial transfer of capital resources as well as human and technical knowhow in the field of banking and payment systems management. In this regard, it is significant that Deutsche and Dresdner Bank have transferred some 1 600 of their own people to eastern Germany to manage the startup process and provide management training. Other German banks, including the Union of German Savings Banks, are engaged in similar, though less extensive, transfers of banking skills and knowhow.

What practical implications are suggested by eastern German experiences for other central and eastern European countries? Given the limited time since the date of the reforms, any list is inevitably tentative:

i) Financial market reform and enterprise privatisation must be closely co-ordinated and follow a clear set of priorities. This is essential in order to minimise the fiscal costs of such reforms – no other central and eastern European country can anticipate the abundant external support enjoyed by eastern Germany for its reform efforts.

ii) The setting of priorities for cleaning up enterprise balance sheets and financial reforms must begin with the adoption of audits using western accounting methodology that permits the government to rank enterprises and bank loans from the best to the worst.

iii) The recapitalisation of the banking system should create an institutional structure to manage the "work-out" of old restructured loans; access to new credits should be tied to the enterprises' servicing of old loans according to their abilities.

iv) The rapid creation of a modern commercial banking system is feasible only if human skills and knowhow can be transferred quickly and on a significant scale. This seems unlikely unless countries are willing to grant interested foreign banks a significant domestic banking franchise without the legacy of past bad corporate debts.

The eastern German experience also serves to highlight the considerable economic risks that western banks opening new branches or subsidiaries in central and eastern Europe are likely to encounter in any domestic lending activity during the transition to market-based economies. The banks' caution could rule out a substantial near-term role for foreign private banks in efforts to recast the existing banking system. Although the many new financial sector investments undertaken by western banks will have clear positive benefits, these ventures will not come close in the aggregate to matching the scope of western German involvement in eastern German financial markets.

This suggests that financial market restructuring in central and eastern Europe could be viewed as a necessary precondition for the successful and rapid transfer of western capital into commercial banking in these economies. Whether such a role for foreign capital in the banking industry is desirable or not is up to the individual countries to decide.

In the absence of such a decision, government involvement in financial sector management will continue strong; privatisation of existing financial institutions does not appear feasible in the short run. What is important is that central and eastern European authorities initiate the restructuring process as soon as clear priorities can be determined. The contribution of foreign capital in the banking industry may be expected to grow once progress in implementing key structural reforms is evident.

Notes

1. Roberto de Rezende Rocha, "Structural Adjustment and Inflation in Yugoslavia", World Bank, EMTTF Division, 26 May 1989, p. 6.
2. Fernando Saldanha, "Interest Rate Subsidies and Monetization in Poland", World Bank, EMTTF Division, April 1989, p. 2.
3. Data cited by Mitja Gaspari, Deputy Governor, National Bank of Yugoslavia in a private meeting with commercial banks in New York. If contingent liabilities of the banks are included (mostly guarantees granted at the request of Yugoslav firms) the potential losses would be increased further.
4. The National Bank of Hungary is currently addressing these problems in the context of a financial sector modernisation loan from the World Bank. The NBH is conducting audits of all the commercial banks according to GAAP and there are plans to send a new banking law to Parliament by the end of 1990.
5. Jeffrey Sachs, "What is to Be Done?" *The Economist,* 13 January 1990.
6. In his article (cited above) Sachs does not even address the problem of setting up functioning markets for labour and capital.
7. "Poland Says Free Market Reached, Austerity to Ease", *Reuters,* 6 June 1990.
8. "Radical options for privatisations", *Financial Times,* 2 August 1990.
9. Sachs, "What is to Be Done?" pp. 21-25.
10. The Hungarian Government reduced its share holding in its three large commercial banks to just over 50 per cent by selling off bank shares to enterprises. The banks in other countries remain wholly state-owned.
11. There is a close parallel in this regard with the Savings and Loan crisis in the United States. It was possible for the Reagan administration to paper over such losses for quite a long time. But when a decision was made by President Bush to deal with the problem, the accumulated losses had to be covered with real resources from the budget. Most experts believe the U.S. Treasury paid a much higher price by deferring a solution to the problem for so long. It is also very difficult to estimate the scope of potential losses in such a situation until the assets in question are sold off or written down to actual value. There is a strong political inclination to understate the actual losses likely to be realised.
12. I fully agree with this characterisation of the banks outlined by Manuel Hinds in his paper, "Issues in the Introduction of Market Forces in Eastern European Socialist Economies", World Bank, EMTTF Division, March 1990, p. 11.
13. In Poland, the debt is carried on the books of the Bank Handlowy, while in Yugoslavia, the debt is carried both by the commercial banks and the National Bank. In Bulgaria, most of the foreign debt is on the books of the Bulgarian Foreign Trade Bank.
14. Hinds, "Issues", p. 14.
15. Rocha, "Structural Adjustment", p. 6.
16. Rocha, "Structural Adjustments", p. 31.

17. Any decision to socialise a portion of a firm's losses prior to privatisation should be transparent in the sense that the social costs and benefits of such actions should be made public and be subject to review by competent authorities.

18. Hinds, "Issues", p. 57. Hinds provides an excellent discussion of the reasons why bank recapitalisations are desirable.

19. This option was recommended by the Blue Ribbon Commission, which prepared an "Action Program" for Hungary's new democratic government, *Hungary – In Transformation to Freedom and Prosperity: Economic Program Proposals of the Joint Hungarian-International Blue Ribbon Commission*, Indianapolis: Hudson Institute, Inc., April 1990, pp. 28-29.

20. "E. German banking costs soar", *Financial Times*, 28 June 1990, p. 33. Deutsche Bank acquired 122 Kreditbank branches and Dresdner Bank took over 72 bank offices; in addition, both banks are in the process of opening a handful of their own branches on eastern German territory, primarily in Berlin. Both banks acquired a 49 per cent share in their ventures; Deutsche Bank later increased its share to 84.7 per cent by injecting a further DM 700 million into its venture. "Deutsche Bank ups stake in Kreditbank venture," *Financial Times*, 24 July 1990.

21. "E. German Kreditbank Chief Against Dissolution", *Reuters*, 15 August 1990.

22. "Bonn To Propose Debt Moratorium for E. German Firms", *Reuters*, 20 August 1990. According to the proposal, the debt of the corporate sector would be addressed as a separate clause of the German unity treaty. In the meantime, the Treuhandanstalt, the eastern German agency responsible for the corporate sector and privatisation, would determine which firms are to benefit from formal debt forgiveness. In all probability, the bulk of the debt will have to be written off entirely. How the costs of such writeoffs are to accounted for in budget terms is as yet unknown.

23. "Kohl calls in W. German bankers", *Financial Times*, 9 August 1990.

Structural Conditions for a Stable Monetary Régime and Efficient Allocation of Investment: Soviet Country Study

Wolfram Schrettl

Introduction

The monetary regime of Soviet-type economies has been a neglected subject for a long time, both inside and outside the relevant countries. However, interest in monetary matters has gradually increased, until all observers have come to understand that "money matters" in socialism. Recent efforts to transfer centrally planned economies into market economies has drawn even more attention to monetary policy. This paper sketches changes in the Soviet monetary system that need to be implemented to allow for a successful transformation of the economy.

Implicit and explicit suggestions are made against a contemporary background in which there is a dramatic deterioration of the Soviet economic situation and its further prospects. One may argue that neither the economic *status quo* nor its dynamics are quite as bad as Soviet observers and events seem to tell us. However, the present author is convinced that the ongoing situation is dramatic. Therefore, special consideration has been given to the aspect of time needed to implement policy measures. In fact, no effort is made to concoct any new clever systemic schemes; no grand novelties are suggested; and the recommendations do not describe an elegant and orderly transition. Rather my recommendations indicate the need to engage in a "quick and possibly dirty" operation.

The sources from which the present paper derived some inspiration were mainstream economics and the experiences of the ongoing reform processes in Poland[1] and eastern Germany (German Democratic Republic before the unification of Germany)[2]. Both economies provide most valuable learning and testing grounds for the larger task, the transformation of the Soviet economy.

On the conditions for a successful transformation

Past attempts to overcome the flaws of the Soviet economy focused first on "perfecting"[3] the traditional command system. Subsequent references began to incorporate more "market elements" into the system of central allocation. As is well known, there never was any clearly identifiable positive effect. My interpretation of the Soviet discussions on economic reform is that only recently has the aim of the reform measures changed in a fundamental way. The almost-fully-declared objective

109

is to introduce a "competitive capitalist democracy"[4], no matter what sort of rhetorical packaging is being applied.

It is a fundamental assumption[5] of the present paper that going "all the way" to a competitive capitalist democracy is the only promising recipe for a successful economic reform of the Soviet (or any Soviet-type) economy. Any hesitation along the way is bound to lead to failure: institutional elements of a market type will remain "empty institutional shells" unable to fulfil any of the expectations connected with their establishment as long as economic reforms fall short of the creation of a full-fledged market economy.

Although the view expounded in the above paragraph may be regarded as a theoretical insight, it would help save us a lot of energy if we looked at it as an empirical regularity. In view of the present Soviet problematique it may nevertheless be worthwhile to make explicit one or two of the theoretical considerations underlying our point of view.

On corruption

Let us first look at the phenomenon of corruption. Corruption is known to be pervasive in the Soviet economy. In Soviet-type systems in general, the full extent of corruption usually becomes known only after the fall of a given regime. While the moral outrage in those countries may be understandable, it does not properly address the core of the issue. In the economic literature, corruption is seen in imperfections of the competitive process. In the Soviet context, it is more useful to focus on the aspect of ownership. Allocation of resources in the Soviet economy is, at least much more frequently than in Western economies, made by non-owners. The allocation of resources by non-owners increases the possibility and likelihood of corruption because non-owners receive at most a fraction of the gains in income and wealth created by their decisions. Efforts to avoid the emergence of such behaviour are costly and thus can never be comprehensive. In short, the need to base the new Soviet reform squarely on private ownership of resources may not only be justified by traditional arguments, such as proper evaluation of risk or establishment of wealth incentives (rather than only income incentives), but also by the need to eliminate misallocation of resources due to corruption[6].

On democracy

A second theoretical consideration focuses on the economic role of democracy. One frequently encounters, also in Western discussions, a certain neglect of the relation between politics and the time horizon of entrepreneurial decision making. This amounts to a careless switch from assuming an unchanged political environment to assuming the latter's unimportance (from *ceteris paribus* to *ceteris levibus,* so to speak). If entrepreneurial decisions are to be made with the proper long-run perspective, then entrepreneurs need to have equally long-run confidence into the rules of the economic game. Democracy can provide a sufficiently long time horizon[7].

At the same time, democracy bestows upon any government the legitimacy necessary to implement radical measures. It is well known that Soviet advisors expressed their envy vis-a-vis Poland on precisely that point, and rightly so. A new alliance between the centre and the republics or, more specifically, the one between Gorbachev and Yeltsin that now appears to have emerged[8], may be helpful in the direction of legitimacy. From this perspective, it remains to be seen whether genuine free elections can temporarily be avoided. I am inclined to believe not, certainly not in the longer run. Over a short-term horizon, with the new reform package finally agreed upon, the coalition behind the reform will need credibility. The full legal underpinnings for the new reform are unlikely to be in place in time, at least not in an operational sense. So there needs to be a credible commitment on the part of the reformers that the reform is going to be pushed through. This commitment is of crucial importance for individual economic agents, including foreign ones, whose behaviour is a direct function of that commitment. The persistence of wait-and-see-attitudes can do considerable damage. In Poland and even in the eastern Germany, despite all those headlines to the contrary, such attitudes still prevail and are very hard to overcome[9]. That seems to suggest that the utmost needs to be done in the Soviet Union to build up the confidence both of the domestic and the international investors' community in the sincerity and persistence of the reform effort.

While the above remarks on corruption and on democracy were meant to suggest the need for a well-functioning market economy, with both private ownership[10] of resources and political democracy, in the end we began to make recommendations. This may be quite appropriate on specific points. However, on issues of a general character we tend to hold the view that, further recommendations are unnecessary at the present stage. In particular, we assume that the leadership has understood the inevitability of *i)* multi-party democracy, *ii)* private ownership of resources up to a "critical mass"[11], including ownership by foreigners, i.e. foreign direct investment[12], *iii)* a complete set of markets (in a macroeconomic sense, i.e. comprising markets for goods, land, labour, and capital[13]).

This also means that the Soviet Union cannot afford much further tinkering with socialism – other than for rhetorical purposes, as long as it remains a necessity to assuage some segments of the population[14]. Thus, the task for the Soviet leadership is now to establish something like a working market economy of the Western type[15] and, in addition, to do so at a pace that helps to cushion the ongoing economic collapse.

On sequencing

In the newly developing tradition of studies on the "transformation" of planned economies, the sequence of reform steps is given considerable attention. The discussion is mostly confined to how to sequence the liberalisation of macroeconomic markets (for goods, land, labour, capital, and foreign exchange). Particular sequences are thought to differ with respect to the sum of disadvantages they generate. A preferred sequence appears to be the one that minimises the sum of these disadvantages[16]. While sequencing may be of some importance, the Polish and eastern German examples seem to indicate that *i)* speedy implementation of individual measures, *ii)* reduction of the time-intervals between the individual measures, *iii)* speedy correction of policy mistakes, and *iv)* doing well whatever is being done[17] may be of overriding practical importance.

A major justification for this relative neglect of the sequencing issue is found in the political context of the transformation process. The opponents of a complete transition to a market system have rallied, for lack of a viable alternative, behind gradualist slogans. The arguments and policies of gradualism put issues of equity at centre stage, as if the goal, now that socialism is gone, were to find at least a "socialist path to capitalism". If one does not consider that search futile, one should at least be aware that to strengthen gradualism may de facto mean to strengthen the opponents of a transition, those who use the sequencing discussion as a pretext, if not for preventing change, then at least for doing nothing at all or as a red herring for the naive.

From an analytic point of view, it may be questionable whether an optimal sequence can be identified in a theoretically and empirically satisfying way. Moreoever, institutional change itself is endogenous. Thus, if distortions are indeed created by a "wrong" sequence of measures, then these distortions serve also as a powerful incentive to "fill the gaps" in a given set of incomplete reform measures. The relative absence of glaring gaps could in effect slow down progress.

Finally, the emphasis on speed in the implementation of the transition is not only motivated by the desire to eliminate allocative inefficiency in the traditional sense but also (and even more) by the conviction that, under contemporary Soviet circumstances, arbitrage opportunities created by gaps in the transition process are unlikely to remain unused for very long. In other words, policing limited liberalisation of markets appears to be next to impossible, resulting in a wealth of undesirable developments[18].

On the elimination of the monetary overhang

Whatever the views on the issue of sequencing may be, elimination of the monetary overhang, whose existence nobody questions anymore, is invariably considered one of the essential elements of any reform package. The origins of the overhang can be traced back to a number of policies of the recent past, i.e. mostly during the second half of the eighties. Thus, Gorbachev's early attempts at "acceleration" by modernisation included, inter alia, that priority was given, up to and including 1988, to investment rather than to consumption (with nominal wage growth continuing as before). Furthermore, the growth of defence expenditures continued undiminished (also up to and including 1988), and then there was of course the infamous anti-alcohol-campaign which reduced supply and redirected demand to alternatives.

Several reasons contributed to the authorities' loss of control over wage-growth. One of them is the rapidly expanding network of cooperatives that has managed to bridge effectively the gap between the two "monies", i.e. the accounting money used for inter-enterprise payments and the cash used for transactions between the firm/ state and the household sectors. As a result, the monetary overhang in the enterprise sphere has begun to add to the overhang in the hands of the population.

The size of aggregate excess demand on the consumer goods market is unknown, though most estimates put it at somewhat over 160 billion rubles, roughly one third of annual (constrained) consumption expenditures. The total stock of savings that could turn into potential demand amounts to an estimated 400 to 500 billion rubles. If present trends of disposable income and production continue, the aggregate excess demand will continue to increase[19].

112

A political aspect

It is worth noting that the monetary overhang creates problems for both the traditional command system and any conceivable new market system. The elimination of the overhang is a precondition for the effective functioning of a market system, but it also rehabilitates to some extent the environment needed for the functioning of the old command system. Therefore, the precise method of reducing the monetary overhang may also have some political significance. In particular, siphoning off the overhang too early, i.e. before further progress towards market reforms has been secured politically, may undermine the transformation process[20]. It is not surprising, therefore, that Soviet proponents of the old system tend to favour methods of eliminating the overhang that do not further destroy the command economy, especially a currency reform[21]. Other methods, such as price liberalisation of the Polish type, or massive privatisation, such as envisaged by Petrakov *et al.* in early summer of 1990 and later included in the reform package of Shatalin *et al.*[22], have the advantage of also overcoming and replacing a significant part of the command system.

Techniques

The elimination of the monetary overhang, via a currency reform appears to have been ruled out already. This was probably a wise decision, not only because of the political risk mentioned above, but also because under contemporary Soviet conditions it would be impossible to maintain secrecy about the preparations for a currency reform. As a result, the willingness to keep ruble-balances would be reduced to zero (or at least to vastly lower levels than even now). In the meantime, the likely consequences for the real sector of the economy would be disastrous.

As to the other two principal methods of eliminating the monetary overhang, price increases (administrative or by price liberalisation) or an increase in supply (consumer goods and assets), the most important point seems to be that neither approach can be successful without being followed almost immediately by the other. Price increases may be enacted in the form of a "shock therapy", characterised by a radical price liberalisation (including abolition or at least a significant reduction of most subsidies) combined with a restrictive monetary (and fiscal) policy[23], which, in the Polish case, has successfully eliminated the monetary overhang. Of course, Polish elimination of the monetary overhang included a final burst of hyperinflation, lasting a little more than two months.

Alternatively, price increases may be enacted in an administrative way as envisaged in the original Ryzhkov (All-Union) Government plan. The political drawback of this approach has already been outlined above. Incidentally, an improvement on both variants of price increases may be to combine an initial administrative increase of prices, say a doubling, followed immediately by subsequent price liberalisation. If done properly, that may not only avoid the above-mentioned political risk, but it may also save the economy the two to three months it takes to get through the period of (hyper-) inflationary adjustment.

In any case, the Polish example demonstrates that radical price liberalisation, if not immediately accompanied by an equally radical change of other aspects of the economic system, may yield disappointing results. More specifically, much too timid plans were envisaged for the privatisation of state enterprises and the development of capital markets (including commercial banks). As a result, a recession is unfolding, characterised by sharply increasing unemployment, sharply declining real incomes, an almost non-existent "supply reaction" and precious little private foreign investment. The Polish Government and its international (credit-giving) advisors are now struggling to speed up, as can be seen from the heightened privatisation activity and the attempt to mount for the commercial banking system an effort similar to the one currently under way for the central bank.

The Polish example seems to reveal the weakness of asymmetric "shock-therapy" (a radical brake on inflation, but a slow change of the system's institutions). At the same time, one should recognise that price liberalisation combined with restrictive monetary policy at least creates pressure on the government to avoid the deepening and eventual perpetuation of what is euphemistically called a "transitory" recession.

The elimination of the monetary overhang through increased supply as envisaged in the original Shatalin plan, i.e. privatisation, de-monopolisation and other institutional reforms to be introduced before price liberalisation, also has drawbacks. As far as elimination of the monetary overhang is concerned, it is for all practical purposes impossible ever to sell enough company shares to the general public so that the latter eventually stops forming queues for milk and meat. In particular, the structure of prices cannot possibly be rationalised in this way. But it then will also be very hard to determine exactly when the aggregate monetary overhang has successfully been eliminated[24]. In other words, there is no way to avoid freeing prices at some point. That, too, will result in considerable inflationary adjustment[25]. Thus, implementing institutional reforms first, i.e. before price liberalisation, is not a promising way to avoid a shock to the price-level – and can of course never be a way to prevent a shock to the structure of relative prices.

Furthermore, privatisation does take some time. What are Soviet entrepreneurs expected to do with the newly acquired companies? The continuation of production at loss-making prices until institutional reforms are eventually completed is unlikely. Either subsidies will have to continue or the enterprises are going to be closed down right away (if buyers can be found for them, under such conditions, in the first place). In the latter case, unemployment will result. The question has to be raised at this point, what sort of unemployment/recession is to be preferred: unemployment resulting from moving toward a market-clearing structure of relative prices (in the admittedly limited Polish sense) or unemployment resulting from an obviously not market-clearing structure of relative prices. Such an "irrational" structure of relative prices would prevail under the Shatalin plan, but clearly also under the Ryzhkov plan of an administrative increase (let's say doubling) of present Soviet prices. If unemployment is really unavoidable, then it should at least affect the "right" producers, those who either do not meet the demand or do so inefficiently. In particular, the Shatalin plan may result in the "wrong" type of unemployment.

A further consideration is that the Shatalin-approach contains a "time-bomb". If privatisation and demonopolisation are to be implemented first, then price liberalisation will almost invariably mean price increases of the goods produced by the newly privatised firms. The angry reaction of the Soviet public to the relatively small-scale problem of co-operative prices should suffice to demonstrate the potentially explosive political side-effects of such an approach.

114

The alternative approaches of Ryzhkov (administrative prices increases) and of Poland (price liberalisation) look from this perspective more attractive. In either case, the initial price increases after price reform would be introduced by *state* enterprises. The ensuing privatisation (assumed it comes at all and, furthermore, does so sufficiently fast) can be expected to drive down the prices initially raised by state enterprises. Consequently, the dramatic initial (administrative or market-driven) hyperinflation cannot be blamed on the newly privatised enterprises. In the Soviet Union, putting the blame on the government rather than on "new capitalists" could prove quite helpful politically. In general, one would expect a major impediment to such a procedure to be the difficulty for a government lacking sufficient legitimacy to introduce radical price liberalisation in the first place. In the specific Soviet case, it was the government that favoured price increases and it was the president who shied away from them, at least for the time being and at least partly[26]. If a (hyper-) inflationary adjustment were to take place in the Soviet Union "by default", as one may expect in the wake of administrative increase in wholesale prices, then this does not necessarily have to be seen in quite so negative terms (as most observers seem to do now). A bigger problem may rather emerge from a relative absence of complementary systemic change, like in the Polish case[27].

Elements of a workable financial infrastructure

It is widely accepted that no matter how the monetary overhang is going to be eliminated, some "transitory" recession will almost inevitably emerge. Among the conditions that will then need to be either in place already or will have to be developed within a short time-span, the existence of a complete set of (macroeconomic) markets has already been mentioned. In this section, we shall focus on some aspects of the infrastructure necessary for a workable financial sector.

The present soon-to-be-replaced Soviet banking system came into being partly as the result of a July-1987 decree. It was implemented from 1988 when the old "monobank", Gosbank, was split into a residual Gosbank and a number of sector-specific, non-competing banks[28]. That development had little to do with a market-oriented two-level banking system. However, as a consequence of the 1987 reform the number of "bankers" in the country seems to have increased substantially, judging by some complaints about "newly created bureaucracies". From this perspective, the 1987 reform may have been a useful intermediate step towards building up at least some of the staff and some of the qualifications needed for modern banking. A second development, falling into the period after the old monobank system, is the mushrooming of small "commercial" and "co-operative" banks. Although they number several hundred already, their quantitative significance is still minuscule[29].

The approach taken in the Soviet Union to banking system reform parallels those already under way in other emerging market economies. Thus, present Soviet plans, though still on the drawing board, include the formation of a two-level banking system[30]. There can be little doubt anymore, that a Western-type central bank is to be established which is intended to conduct an independent monetary policy. At the same time, genuine commercial banks are to be created which should compete against each other both regarding deposits and credits. Unfortunately, it is much easier to decree such a banking system than it is to ensure its proper functioning. The problems relate both to the internal organisation of the newly created banks and to the characteristics of the economic environment in which they operate.

Central bank

Concerning the modernisation of the functions and operations of Gosbank, it appears indispensable that the Soviet Union rely on the experience of Western central banks. The relevant know-how is concentrated in those institutions, rather than being spread widely. As is well-known, there exists a procedure that is presently being applied to the Polish central bank, and thus at least has been tested to a certain extent. There, the International Monetary Fund (IMF) is co-ordinating technical assistance by half a dozen Western central banks in different areas: banking supervision, money market and short term securities (as instruments of monetary policy), monetary and balance of payments research, payments system, foreign exchange market operations, internal accounting and audit procedures, and so forth. In the Soviet case, the prevailing urgency of the problems argues in favour of the "proven Polish method". However, full use of IMF resources is impossible until the Soviet Union becomes a member of the IMF. At the same time, it is conceivable that the individual Western central banks would have mounted the necessary effort even without the co-ordinating activity of the IMF. However, one may question the willingness of each individual bank to join the effort due, for example, to concern that participation in such a project would have posed major political issues for the banks. Nonetheless, various signals indicate that such an uncoordinated effort was already under way well before the Houston Summit cleared the path towards direct involvement of the IMF, OECD, World Bank, and EBRD.

Given the experience Western central bankers have acquired as a consequence of their involvement in Poland, it seems feasible that the Soviet operation can be successfully completed within an even shorter period of time. However, this would only apply to issues such as accounting standards (both for internal purposes and for dealings with future commercial banks), and other relatively technical problems (including hardware and software). A more difficult task concerns the quality and quantity of the available staff. The experiences gathered by the Bundesbank in eastern Germany indicate that, with few exceptions, the training of the eastern German central bank staff leaves a lot to be desired. As a result, the Bundesbank found it indispensable to deploy a total of roughly 300 of its own staff into eastern Germany, reportedly occupying completely the upper ranks in the respective hierarchy. While this is an extreme example, it suggests that the required deployment of Western central banks' staff might run into the thousands if a fully water-tight effort were to become necessary in the Soviet Union. Deployment of Western central bank personnel on such a scale appears to be unlikely. Rather, this example provides an upper bound on any potential Western staff requirements.

Even harder than the training of the personnel will be the problem of establishing the credibility and the reputation of a Soviet central bank. As is well known, these seemingly intangible factors are crucial to the effectiveness of central bank policy. Soviet plans aim at giving the central bank an independent status, which should prevent the government from financing budget deficits by the "printing press" and from appropriating deposits in savings banks. It remains to be seen, of course, how far these intentions will be put into practice.

116

The method now discussed, and incorporated in the draft laws on banking, is to achieve this objective by subordinating the central bank to the Supreme Soviet (rather than to the government). This appears to be rather less than the ultimate form of independence which, these days, is identified mostly with the Bundesbank. While the construction envisaged now does not preclude a conduct of monetary policy geared towards price stability, the wisdom behind the decision to leave loopholes that potentially allow a continuation of past practice is questionable. Furthermore, while the recent Gorbachev plan contains a provision that explicitly forbids the monetisation of fiscal deficits, it gives at the same time the right to the president to issue "limited" amounts of short-term credit. In any case, the actual policies pursued by the central bank (or by the Supreme Soviet or by President Gorbachev) will quickly show its mettle and allow it to establish credibility (or lack thereof). One possible way[31] to accelerate the build-up of the necessary reputation may be an early clash with the government, ending in a clear victory for the central bank. This alone, however, will not suffice to create the environment necessary for an independent and effective monetary policy. These issues will be discussed later.

Commercial banks

On a formal level, the creation of independent commercial banks can be achieved fairly easily, and is indeed envisaged in the draft law on commercial banking. Thus, commercial banks will presumably be created by decreeing the independence of the existing sectoral banks, plus possibly through a number of new banks. In the Gorbachev plan, the objective is the transformation of the state-owned specialised banks into joint-stock commercial banks. Only the savings bank is to remain under state ownership. The new commercial banks supposedly will not be privately owned but rather "socially owned," thus maintaining "socialist choice." Upon closer inspection, ownership by joint-stock companies, though the shares may be owned by individuals, counts as "social ownership", rather than private ownership, under the new definition of socialism[32]. Shares of the new banks are indeed to be widely held[33]. In any case, a system of "universal" commercial banks is to be established, complemented by a number of specialised institutions such as pension and investment funds, broker and leasing firms, etc. Therefore, it appears that the system will be modelled after the German universal bank system with some elements added from the U.K./ U.S. system.

Of course, many problems remain to be solved. Again, as is the case with the central bank, a number of circumstances internal to the commercial banks will create considerable difficulties. For example, one will be the application of accounting standards to the commercial banks themselves. The importance of the accounting standards derives from the necessity to assess the quality of the banks' assets. Furthermore there are the usual technical problems related to hardware and software as well as the problems of training the banks' staff.

The task differs however from reforming the central bank, not only regarding its precise contents, but more importantly with respect to the larger dimension of the problem. As an indication of this, it may be worthwhile to look at the number of senior officers that western German commercial banks are deploying in eastern Germany. Their total number is a minimum of 1 500. This number includes not only officers of western German banks that have taken stakes in eastern German banks, but also some personnel deployed on a good-will basis by western German savings and co-operative banks. While the example may again be an extreme one, one should nevertheless keep in mind that mounting a similar effort in the Soviet case could require deployment of tens of thousands of Western staff. Clearly, there exist numerous reasons why such an excessive approach is not needed (and even more reasons why it may not be possible). Most importantly, Soviet bankers are already being trained in considerable numbers in the West. I do not have any precise figures, however anecdotal evidence leads me to believe that their number might go into the hundreds. In the wake of the recent agreements[34], the number of Soviet personnel trained in the West should increase sharply.

One of the largest gaps in the qualification profiles of Soviet bankers is likely to be in the area of credit judgement. While this gap clearly needs to be filled, even more serious difficulties will be encountered when applying Western accounting standards to Soviet enterprises seeking credit. Under present conditions, it is virtually impossible to pass judgement on the creditworthiness of Soviet companies, which in turn also makes it extremely hard to evaluate the quality of the assets of Soviet banks. But not only inadequate accounting rules are responsible for the present problems. Other difficulties are related to the lack of market-clearing prices of assets and to the distorted economic behaviour of firms, resulting for example in balance sheets that are typically overloaded with stocks of inputs.

Since balance sheets of Soviet banks contain huge amounts of dubious assets, i.e. bad debt, it will be necessary to write down those assets. The problem is likely to become even more explosive fairly soon. Once a recession begins to unfold in the wake of eliminating the monetary overhang, the number of de-facto-bankrupt companies will sharply increase, with obvious effects on the asset-side of the banks' balance sheets. This problem may be accentuated further by the possibility of an explosive expansion of mutual credit among state enterprises, mostly in the form of more or less involuntary trade credit. Irritatingly enough, the Gorbachev plan calls for an expansion of inter-firm trade credit as a means of reducing bank credit[35].

Similar problems exist in Poland. In the field of Polish commercial banks the World Bank is mounting an effort parallel to the effort of the IMF regarding the Polish central bank. While the IMF's task in principle can be solved rather swiftly, the activities of the World Bank concerning Polish commercial banks will take many years to complete due to the scale of the problem. Should the Soviet Union consider to proceed along lines similar to the Polish example (although it appears unclear so far[36], exactly who in the West would organise such a project), it is highly risky to count on the timely success of such an approach. The risk would be much lower if the Soviet Union were willing to prepare the ground for a more active role of Western commercial banks in the Soviet Union. There are indications that the Soviet Union will follow such a course[37]. It is unclear, however, whether the Soviet Union will do so on a sufficient scale.

In any case, it appears indispensable that the legal framework in which commercial banks are supposed to operate be suitably modified. Most important, ownership rights for land and other property need to be clarified. If commercial banks are expected to act as efficient financial intermediaries, the procedures for access to collateral will need to be well-defined[38]. The crucial importance of stable and well-defined ownership rights has become empirically obvious again in the State and Unity

Treaties in Germany. Such property rights greatly facilitate access to and reduce the cost of credit[39].

The environment for a workable financial infrastructure

The importance of a "complete" set of reform measures for a successful transformation of the Soviet economy has already been spelt out in general terms above. At this point, some of the conditions that need to be fulfilled by the immediate environment of the newly-to-be-established two-level banking system will be clarified in more specific terms.

Collateral and horizontal capital flows

For some time to come, the general economic environment in the Soviet Union (or in the case of independent republics) will be characterised by considerable uncertainty. From a banker's point of view, one of the most damaging uncertainties is the relative lack of reliable ways to assess the creditworthiness of both newly founded and old companies. Unless all horizontal capital flows are to be arranged by way of venture capital, "junk bonds" or personal bank credit, all of them either quite costly or quite limited in potential scope or both, ways must be found to reduce the credit risk as seen from the side of the credit-giving units. The easiest way to convince a banker of even the craziest business idea is to come up with ample collateral. The higher the uncertainty, the more collateral is typically needed.

A simple method to spread potential collateral in the Soviet economy is to increase the "net worth" of individuals or of credit-seeking institutions in general. One may even argue that, other things equal, the uncertainty prevailing in the Soviet economy requires even larger amounts of such "net worth" to facilitate horizontal capital flows than in a well-established market economy, i.e. the necessary "critical mass" of private ownership may have to be even higher. One way to spread the necessary wealth is to privatise state assets "free of charge" in the way discussed in Czechoslovakia[40]. Another way would be to let banks "collect" (from state enterprises, for example) the collateral for non-performing loans and auction it off, thus in effect decentralising the business of privatisation to the new commercial banks (rather than monopolising the task in some privatisation agency).

In any case, one of the most useful assets, when it comes to collateral, is certainly land. It is one of the legacies of the old Soviet system (or any Soviet-type economy) that the value[41] of physical capital is rather limited. Thus, given the relative dearth of other assets that can be privatised under Soviet circumstances, it would be unwise, from the perspective of facilitating horizontal capital flows, not to privatise land[42]. As is well known, privatisation of land is one of the reform measures where Gorbachev, in "his" plan, is said to have balked. On the other hand, the adopted approach by the Soviet Government, i.e. decentralisation to the republics of the decision on the privatisation of land, may well be an effective method of achieving the intended privatisation while at the same time fragmenting the opposition by dispersing its ire over multiple targets. Incidentally, the Gorbachev plan does call for quick implementation of land reform in the republics. Furthermore, the plan calls for fast resolution of the legal problems surrounding the use of land and other property as collateral for obtaining bank credit, in particular credit from foreign banks[43].

Monetary policy: some conditions

An effective monetary policy seems also to be facilitated by accelerated privatisation. As the Polish and earlier Yugoslav cases demonstrate, state-owned companies go much further than privately owned companies towards granting each other trade credits in the event of monetary restriction. Before monetary restrictions become effective, large numbers of enterprises may be ruined financially. As was already mentioned before, the Gorbachev plan indeed envisages expansion of such inter-enterprise trade credits, thus even reinforcing that negative tendency.

A further requirement for a modern banking system to function properly sounds almost too trivial to be mentioned here. However, there have been cases where the independence of a newly established central bank has been solemnly declared without prior creation of the conditions for independent monetary and fiscal policies. If finance ministers in need for funds should not be forced either to empty (in the traditional Soviet *ad hoc* way) the enterprises' or savings banks' coffers or to order the central bank to "print money" (in which case monetary and fiscal policies are automatically conducted *uno actu*), some market-driven "funds-window" should exist, preferably non-distorted markets for money and capital. Thus the establishment of such markets[44] is a *sine qua non* for the functioning of an independent central bank. The easiest way to establish those markets may be to leave the task to the newly-to-be-created commercial banks in conjunction with the other institutions mentioned above, i.e. insurance companies, pension funds, etc. The Gorbachev plan explicitly envisages establishment of the necessary financial markets.

A remark on convertibility

A final issue that attracts considerable attention in the Soviet Union is that of convertibility of the ruble. Originally, Soviet plans seemed to prefer a very slow path to convertibility. More recently, a certain need seems to have been perceived to accelerate the process[45]. However, the Gorbachev plan envisages "internal convertibility" only for the last stage (stage four[46]) of the transition process, with full convertibility to follow "gradually" over some unspecified later period. "Internal convertibility" is understood as comprising convertibility for transactions on current account only (rather than transactions on capital account as well) and only by residents. The definition of resident does however comprise foreign-owned companies. The objective of introducing internal convertibility is to achieve liberalisation of imports while at the same time preventing undesirable capital flows. This path to convertibility is now standard in the emerging market economies and is also in line with the advice given by the IMF to Poland.

One of the fears expressed on the Soviet side in connection with early convertibility is that there would be an outflow of funds from the country. Domestic goods are rightly considered attractive neither to Soviet buyers nor buyers on the world market. On the other hand, Soviet buyers would reveal a large hunger for foreign goods. As a result, it is feared that with a fixed exchange rate the Soviet Union would suffer from loss of hard currency reserves and with a flexible exchange rate the value of the ruble would collapse. These problems occur even when convertibility is only "internal". With full convertibility, a further fear is added, that of capital flight. To avoid either of those outcomes, it is suggested to phase in convertibility slowly. What this involves in detail is not always clear.

Major difficulties with limited convertibility arise from *i)* general contemporary conditions which differ considerably from the frequently cited examples of countries in the West that introduced convertibility only relatively late and *ii)* from specific Soviet conditions. The first factor means that the historical yardstick may be the wrong yardstick. What may matter more with respect to the degree of convertibility is the extent of contemporary competitive pressure on governments. One may argue that competition is much stronger compared to the early post-war period.

The second factor means that it may be extremely difficult to successfully police limited convertibility. It is to be expected that attempts to limit convertibility will necessitate considerable and possibly quite destructive efforts of enforcement. The negative effects may damage the newly emerging market elements in the domestic economy by again nourishing the black market. The milder phenomenon is certainly smuggling of consumer goods, in either direction – depending on the exchange rate. A more serious black market will, however, develop with respect to capital flows. If convertibility is to be limited in that respect, its immediate effect will most likely be to inhibit the inflow of capital. At the same time, numerous possibilities exist (increasing daily with the ever-growing autonomy and ability of Soviet firms to conduct direct foreign trade activities) for capital flight, *inter alia* by hiding away capital flows in current account transactions[47]. Thus, limited convertibility may effectively drain the country of capital resources, especially of the much-desired inflow of non-debt creating private foreign capital.

As to the general Soviet fear of a collapsing ruble in case of convertibility, one may first ask whether this would be such a bad thing. It could be argued that devaluation of the ruble to a level that brings the currency in line with, say, the Polish zloty may actually be helpful. And this is of course the main mechanism for (active or automatic) control of undesirable trade flows. As to the specific Soviet fear of a collapsing ruble in case of convertibility on the capital account, it needs to be confronted with the Soviet fear of foreigners buying up land and companies[48]. If the latter fear is justified, then this implies an upward, rather than a downward, pressure on the foreign exchange value of the ruble. The inflow of foreign capital may also occur as a result of a restrictive monetary policy, i.e. when an interest rate differential, possibly with the expectation of a revaluation, attracts (speculative) funds. In any case, the above observations point to a possibility that appears to be underestimated, i.e. the potential to attain a set of acceptable "equilibria" not only by traditional policy instruments (in particular, monetary and fiscal policy) alone, but rather in conjunction with systemic (reform) policy and most importantly without direct restrictions on capital flows. More specifically, structural changes that attract foreign direct capital may help underpin macroeconomic stability.

The above remarks were less meant to suggest a solution to the problem of convertibility but rather to emphasise two aspects of the issue that are of particular importance in the Soviet context. First, limited convertibility has the potential to create arbitrage problems at least as big as in the worst known cases. The side-effects of limited convertibility may be quite damaging to the newly emerging market system. Second, under the given circumstances, an appropriate way to monitor and control undesirable capital flows may, be found rather in letting them occur as much as possible in the open and trying to react to them with the help of policy instruments that conform to the market-system as an allocation mechanism.

Concluding remarks

The target in the process of transformation of centrally planned economies is rather well defined, both in its general aspects and in the specific aspects discussed in the present paper. From that angle, the process can be described almost exclusively as one of imitation. The possibility of innovation exists more with respect to the precise paths of transformation[49]. There, a considerable degree of uncertainty seems to prevail, some intrinsic, some due to the time pressure[50]. That time pressure is already enormous, and is likely to grow worse as the economy deteriorates and unavoidable errors are made in the transition process. Under such circumstances, the chances of economic "survival" may be significantly enhanced if we conclude that a certain degree of confidence can be placed on the ability of Western commercial banks and financial institutions to speed up the process of creating a workable financial infrastructure. Paving the way for Western commercial banks' and financial institutions' effective involvement in that infrastructure may be the safest bet available to find the amount of privatisation and convertibility required for the effective functioning of the rest of the economy.

Notes

1. Schrettl, "Transition..."
2. Schrettl, "Monetary and Economic Integration..."
3. The notorious *sovershenstovovanie*.
4. That may have been the objective of some crucial players all along, i.e. at least since 1985.
5. Of course, it is an assumption, rather than a result, only for the purposes of the present paper.
6. "Side payments" is the game-theoretic term. More important than language, however, is to see the Soviet reality. Thus, one may safely expect, to give a concrete example, that it is easier to bribe some *Gossnab* official into diverting resources than it is to do the same to a co-operative producer of a given commodity. (Or, to generalise: it's easier to undermine the plan than the market.)
7. "Leftist dictatorships" to do. (Soviet complaints that cooperatives make millions but do not invest all those millions should be seen in that light.) "Rightist dictatorships" may provide a sufficiently long time horizon simply because they may provide 150 per cent security for private property. Ironically, when Western leftists want to demonstrate the feasibility of a market system even without democracy, they frequently refer to right-wing régimes ("Look at South Korea!"). It seems to be harder to give examples of left-wing régimes with a successful market economy. (At the same time it may be necessary, in order not to be misunderstood, to point out that right-wing dictatorships are neither desirable nor, in my view, stable politically, at least not in the long run.)
8. Upon closer inspection, the fierce disagreement with the presidential programme that Yeltsin ("Speech...") expressed in his republic's Supreme Soviet appears to be quite superficial in that he intends to go along with each and every decree and law coming from the union.
9. The process of German unification was, and still is, accompanied by, sometimes desperate, attempts to nail down the crucial factors determining agents' attitudes and expectations, including those regarding ownership rights. This is visible in the State Treaty, in the Unity Treaty, as well as in current political and legal efforts.
10. Clearly, private ownership need not be pervasive. More on the necessary qualifications later.
11. An attempt to make the term less vague will be given later in the paper.
12. For example, Gorbachev, 20 April 1990, and Petrakov, 24 April 1990. In October 1990, a decree and a law were discussed, effectively confirming the earlier announcements.
13. A market for foreign exchange is assumed to be included in that list. Convertibility will be discussed later in the paper.
14. Furthermore, Gorbachev has recently managed to redefine socialism in a way that effectively dissolves it as a stumbling block on the way to capitalism. (Of course, he still rejects capitalism, nominally at least.)

15. Of course, this includes Japan, a more recent role-model (now that Sweden seems to have lost some of its attractiveness to Soviet politicians.)

16. More precisely, trade is to be liberalised early on, together with the introduction of convertibility on current account, in order to expose domestic producers to world market relative prices and competition. Of course, the exchange rate determines the extent of such competition. After liberalism of the goods market follow the labour market, then the capital market, and finally, in the sense of full convertibility, the foreign exchange market. For example, the paper by Pitzner-Jorgensen.

17. This may sound trivial to economists used to selection problems among alternatives along some "production possibility frontier". The ongoing German monetary and economic union demonstrates *iv)* to be a major issue. In general, while it is not so clear which path/ sequence of transition is optimal, it is quite clear that opportunities to fumble loom large along each path. The latter problem may well be weightier than the possible selection of a suboptimal path of transition.

18. See below the remarks on convertibility.

19. For example, most of the players now on centre-stage (e.g. Gorbachev, Rzyhkov, Gos-plan, Shatalin) seem to expect a contraction of output in the first quarter of 1991. The budget deficit according to the Shatalin-plan was to be reduced to zero in 1991. The government-plan, according to Yeltsin's critical interpretation, would result in a 1991 deficit of 300 billion rubles. The Gorbachev plan envisages a deficit of not more than 25 to 30 billion rubles. In other words, there is quite a wide range of possibilities.

20. The 1948 currency reform in Western Germany that wiped out the then existing mone-tary overhang was immediately followed by renewed calls for a continuation and expan-sion of the old administrative control of the economy. Cf. Möller (one of the engineers of the 1948 reform), "Foundations..."

21. Shortly before his ouster, Ligachev had joined the ranks of those demanding a currency reform.

22. Shatalin *et al.* "Transition..."

23. A de-facto wage-freeze was also imposed in the Polish case. However, there is evidence that this constraint may not have been binding.

24. This is not to question the potential use of disequilibrium/quantity rationing/fix-price models, but that the necessary data to apply them will not be available in time.

25. Incidentally, even after the German currency reform of 1948 the rate of inflation increased dangerously. Similarly, there was considerable ex-ante-uncertainty about the extent of transitory inflation after 2 July 1990 in Germany. And it was due to very specific circumstances that inflation did not materialise.

26. The Gorbachev plan envisages massive and early price-increases for "non-essentials".

27. A serious difficulty with inflationary adjustment *per se* may however emerge from a provision in the Gorbachev plan, envisaging indexation not only of wages, etc., but also of savings deposits!

28. *Promstroibank, Agroprombank, Zhilsotsbank, Sberbank,* and *Vneshekonombank.*

29. The volume of outstanding credit at the beginning of 1990 reportedly amounted to about 2 per cent of the banking system's total.

30. In October 1990, the draft laws on the central bank (Gosbank) and on the commercial banks have gone through a first reading in the Supreme Soviet.

31. A doubtful one, I was reminded by A. Blundell-Wignall.

32. Thus, "going public" seems to be interpreted as public ownership.

33. It is stated in the Gorbachev plan that shares should be distributed as widely as possible.

34. Such as the October 1990 agreement between the New York Stock Exchange and the Soviet Ministry of Finance.

35. Fulfilment guaranteed.

36. Notwithstanding a recently declared willingness of the World Bank to become more deeply involved in Soviet problems, even beyond the famous "study" in the wake of the Houston Summit.

37. A further indication of Soviet determination to allow establishment and operations (rather than only representative offices) of Western commercial banks can be seen in the draft law on commercial banks in conjunction with the presidential decree allowing complete foreign ownership of companies.

38. This point will be further discussed later in the paper.

39. Much the same of what has been said here about commercial banks applies mutatis mutandis to other financial institutions such as insurance companies. It is the impression of the present author that there exist both necessity and the possibility for Western insurance companies to play an active role in the Soviet market.

   As a recent development, the Gorbachev plan explicitly calls for insurance companies with foreign participation. Negotiations with Western insurance companies seem to have been under way for quite some time.

40. The coupon-solution.

41. No value here in discussing use versus market versus labour value.

42. Use of leasing appears to be of limited value, from the point of view of its value as collateral for horizontal capital flows, as a substitute for land ownership. However, the difficulties could be partly overcome (though it is hard to see why such detours around private ownership should still be considered). First of all, Soviet plans still do not envisage a secondary market in leasing contracts. If that were allowed, it would make a potentially tremendous difference in the present context. Unfortunately, Gorbachev still seems to be determined to do his utmost to suppress such "speculation". Secondly, in order to provide for a more stable value of a leasing contract, it would be wise, rather than working with a certain length of the lease, say 20 years, to let those 20 years be the *period of notice* before termination of the lease, with the lease itself being principally unlimited.

43. Compare end of section 4 and section 8 of the plan.

44. Of course, at this stage they need not be as sophisticated as Western markets.

45. For example, in the speech on the occasion of presenting his plan, Gorbachev called for the introduction of convertibility in the "near" or "immediate" (*v blizhaishee*) future.

46. No time spans given. However, all four stages are to be completed in "about" (Gorbachev plan) or "at most" (Gorbachev speech) one-and-a-half to two years.

47. In general, the techniques amount simply to over-pricing of imports and under-pricing of exports (in case of capital flight).

48. Of course, similar fears exist in Poland, in Czechoslovakia, and even in the United States.

49. On the interaction between imitation, innovation, and uncertainty as elements in the process of transformation, see Schrettl, "Change of economic systems..."

50. As the saying goes: The necessity to decide exceeds the possibilities to analyse.

References

GORBACHEV, M.S. (1990), "Ob osnovnykh napravleniiach po stabilizatsii narodnogo khoziaistva i perekhodu k rynochnoi ekonomike." *Pravda,* 20 October, (referred to as "Gorbachev Speech").

GORBACHEV, M.S., *et al.* (imputed) (1990), "Osnovnye napravleniia po stabilizatsii narodnogo khoziaistva i perekhodu k rynochnoi ekonomike." *Pravda,* 18 October, (referred to as "Gorbachev plan").

MÖLLER, H. (1988), "Foundations of the German Economic Miracle" (in German). *Neue Zürcher Zeitung,* 19 June.

PITZNER-JORGENSEN, F. (1990), "Economic Reforms and East-West Trade and Cooperation". Paper presented to the 1st Conference of the European Association for Comparative Economic Studies, Verona, 27-29 September.

SCHRETTL, W. "Change of Economic Systems. Fragments for a Theory" (in German). *Schriften des Vereins für Socialpolitik* (forthcoming).

SCHRETTL, W. (1990), "Transition to a Market Economy, Problems of a 'Radical' Model" (in German). *Arbeiten aus dem Osteuropa-Institut München (Working Papers),* No. 137, April. Revised version of a Report to the Prime Minister of Niedersachsen, March.

SCHRETTL, W. "Economic and Monetary Integration of the Two Germanies". *Choix* (forthcoming).

SHATALIN, St., *et al.* (1990) "Transition to the Market, Parts I and II". Moscow, Cultural Initiative Foundation (transl.), August (referred to as "Shatalin Plan").

YELTSIN, B. (1990), Speech in the Supreme Soviet of the Russian Federation. Radio Moscow, 16 October.

WHERE TO OBTAIN OECD PUBLICATIONS – OÙ OBTENIR LES PUBLICATIONS DE L'OCDE

Argentina – Argentine
CARLOS HIRSCH S.R.L.
Galería Güemes, Florida 165, 4° Piso
1333 Buenos Aires   Tel. 30.7122, 331.1787 y 331.2391
Telegram: Hirsch-Baires
Telex: 21112 UAPE-AR. Ref. s/2901
Telefax:(1)331-1787

Australia – Australie
D.A. Book (Aust.) Pty. Ltd.
648 Whitehorse Road, P.O.B 163
Mitcham, Victoria 3132   Tel. (03)873.4411
Telefax: (03)873.5679

Austria – Autriche
OECD Publications and Information Centre
Schedestrasse 7
D-W 5300 Bonn 1 (Germany)   Tel. (49.228)21.60.45
Telefax: (49.228)26.11.04
Gerold & Co.
Graben 31
Wien 1   Tel. (0222)533.50.14

Belgium – Belgique
Jean De Lannoy
Avenue du Roi 202
B-1060 Bruxelles   Tel. (02)538.51.69/538.08.41
Telex: 63220   Telefax: (02) 538.08.41

Canada
Renouf Publishing Company Ltd.
1294 Algoma Road
Ottawa, ON K1B 3W8   Tel. (613)741.4333
Telex: 053-4783   Telefax: (613)741.5439
Stores:
61 Sparks Street
Ottawa, ON K1P 5R1   Tel. (613)238.8985
211 Yonge Street
Toronto, ON M5B 1M4   Tel. (416)363.3171
Federal Publications
165 University Avenue
Toronto, ON M5H 3B8   Tel. (416)581.1552
Telefax: (416)581.1743
Les Publications Fédérales
1185 rue de l'Université
Montréal, PQ H3B 3A7   Tel.(514)954-1633
Les Éditions La Liberté Inc.
3020 Chemin Sainte-Foy
Sainte-Foy, PQ G1X 3V6   Tel. (418)658.3763
Telefax: (418)658.3763

Denmark – Danemark
Munksgaard Export and Subscription Service
35, Nørre Søgade, P.O. Box 2148
DK-1016 København K   Tel. (45 33)12.85.70
Telex: 19431 MUNKS DK   Telefax: (45 33)12.93.87

Finland – Finlande
Akateeminen Kirjakauppa
Keskuskatu 1, P.O. Box 128
00100 Helsinki   Tel. (358 0)12141
Telex: 125080   Telefax: (358 0)121.4441

France
OECD/OCDE
Mail Orders/Commandes par correspondance:
2, rue André-Pascal
75775 Paris Cédex 16   Tel. (33-1)45.24.82.00
Bookshop/Librairie:
33, rue Octave-Feuillet
75016 Paris   Tel. (33-1)45.24.81.67
    (33-1)45.24.81.81
Telex: 620 160 OCDE
Telefax: (33-1)45.24.85.00 (33-1)45.24.81.76
Librairie de l'Université
12a, rue Nazareth
13100 Aix-en-Provence   Tel. 42.26.18.08
Telefax : 42.26.63.26

Germany – Allemagne
OECD Publications and Information Centre
Schedestrasse 7
D-W 5300 Bonn 1   Tel. (0228)21.60.45
Telefax: (0228)26.11.04

Greece – Grèce
Librairie Kauffmann
28 rue du Stade
105 64 Athens   Tel. 322.21.60
Telex: 218187 LIKA Gr

Hong Kong
Swindon Book Co. Ltd.
13 - 15 Lock Road
Kowloon, Hong Kong   Tel. 366.80.31
Telex: 50 441 SWIN HX   Telefax: 739.49.75

Iceland – Islande
Mál Mog Menning
Laugavegi 18, Pósthólf 392
121 Reykjavik   Tel. 15199/24240

India – Inde
Oxford Book and Stationery Co.
Scindia House
New Delhi 110001   Tel. 331.5896/5308
Telex: 31 61990 AM IN
Telefax: (11)332.5993
17 Park Street
Calcutta 700016   Tel. 240832

Indonesia – Indonésie
Pdii-Lipi
P.O. Box 269/JKSMG/88
Jakarta 12790   Tel. 583467
Telex: 62 875

Ireland – Irlande
TDC Publishers – Library Suppliers
12 North Frederick Street
Dublin 1   Tel. 744835/749677
Telex: 33530 TDCP EI   Telefax: 748416

Italy – Italie
Libreria Commissionaria Sansoni
Via Benedetto Fortini, 120/10
Casella Post. 552
50125 Firenze   Tel. (055)64.54.15
    Telefax: (055)64.12.57
Via Bartolini 29
20155 Milano   Tel. 36.50.83
La diffusione delle pubblicazioni OCSE viene assicurata
dalle principali librerie ed anche da:
Editrice e Libreria Herder
Piazza Montecitorio 120
00186 Roma   Tel. 679.46.28
Telex: NATEL I 621427
Libreria Hoepli
Via Hoepli 5
20121 Milano   Tel. 86.54.46
Telex: 31.33.95   Telefax: (02)805.28.86
Libreria Scientifica
Dott. Lucio de Biasio 'Aeiou'
Via Meravigli 16
20123 Milano   Tel. 805.68.98
Telex: 800175

Japan – Japon
OECD Publications and Information Centre
Landic Akasaka Building
2-3-4 Akasaka, Minato-ku
Tokyo 107   Tel. (81.3)3586.2016
Telex: (81.3)3584.7929

Korea – Corée
Kyobo Book Centre Co. Ltd.
P.O. Box 1658, Kwang Hwa Moon
Seoul   Tel. (REP)730.78.91
Telefax: 735.0030

Malaysia/Singapore – Malaisie/Singapour
Co-operative Bookshop Ltd.
University of Malaya
P.O. Box 1127, Jalan Pantai Baru
59700 Kuala Lumpur
Malaysia   Tel. 756.5000/756.5425
Telefax: 757.3661
Information Publications Pte. Ltd.
Pei-Fu Industrial Building
24 New Industrial Road No. 02-06
Singapore 1953   Tel. 283.1786/283.1798
Telefax: 284.8875

Netherlands – Pays-Bas
SDU Uitgeverij
Christoffel Plantijnstraat 2
Postbus 20014
2500 EA's-Gravenhage   Tel. (070 3)78.99.11
Voor bestellingen: Tel. (070 3)78.98.80
Telex: 32486 stdru   Telefax: (070 3)47.63.51

New Zealand – Nouvelle-Zélande
GP Publications Ltd.
Customer Services
33 The Esplanade - P.O. Box 38-900
Petone, Wellington
Tel. (04)685-555   Telefax: (04)685-333

Norway – Norvège
Narvesen Info Center – NIC
Bertrand Narvesens vei 2
P.O. Box 6125 Etterstad
0602 Oslo 6   Tel. (02)57.33.00
Telex: 79668 NIC N   Telefax: (02)68.19.01

Pakistan
Mirza Book Agency
65 Shahrah Quaid-E-Azam
Lahore 3   Tel. 66839
Telex: 44886 UBL PK. Attn: MIRZA BK

Portugal
Livraria Portugal
Rua do Carmo 70-74
Apart. 2681
1117 Lisboa Codex   Tel.: 347.49.82/3/4/5
Telefax: (01) 347.02.64

Singapore/Malaysia – Singapour/Malaisie
See Malaysia/Singapore" – Voir «Malaisie/Singapour»

Spain – Espagne
Mundi-Prensa Libros S.A.
Castelló 37, Apartado 1223
Madrid 28001   Tel. (91) 431.33.99
Telex: 49370 MPLI   Telefax: 575.39.98
Libreria Internacional AEDOS
Consejo de Ciento 391
08009-Barcelona   Tel. (93) 301.86.15
Telefax: (93) 317.01.41

Sri Lanka
Centre for Policy Research
c/o Mercantile Credit Ltd.
55, Janadhipathi Mawatha
Colombo 1   Tel. 438471-9, 440346
Telex: 21138 VAVALEX CE   Telefax: 94.1.448900

Sweden – Suède
Fritzes Fackboksföretaget
Box 16356
Regeringsgatan 12
103 27 Stockholm   Tel. (08)23.89.00
Telex: 12387   Telefax: (08)20.50.21
Subscription Agency/Abonnements:
Wennergren-Williams AB
Nordenflychtsvägen 74
Box 30004
104 25 Stockholm   Tel. (08)13.67.00
Telex: 19937   Telefax: (08)618.62.32

Switzerland – Suisse
OECD Publications and Information Centre
Schedestrasse 7
D-W 5300 Bonn 1 (Germany)   Tel. (49.228)21.60.45
Telefax: (49.228)26.11.04
Librairie Payot
6 rue Grenus
1211 Genève 11   Tel. (022)731.89.50
Telex: 28356
Subscription Agency – Service des Abonnements
Naville S.A.
7, rue Lévrier
1201 Genève   Tél.: (022) 732.24.00
Telefax: (022) 738.48.03
Maditec S.A.
Chemin des Palettes 4
1020 Renens/Lausanne   Tel. (021)635.08.65
Telefax: (021)635.07.80
United Nations Bookshop/Librairie des Nations-Unies
Palais des Nations
1211 Genève 10   Tel. (022)734.60.11 (ext. 48.72)
Telex: 289696 (Attn: Sales)   Telefax: (022)733.98.79

Taiwan – Formose
Good Faith Worldwide Int'l. Co. Ltd.
9th Floor, No. 118, Sec. 2
Chung Hsiao E. Road
Taipei   Tel. 391.7396/391.7397
Telefax: (02) 394.9176

Thailand – Thaïlande
Suksit Siam Co. Ltd.
1715 Rama IV Road, Samyan
Bangkok 5   Tel. 251.1630

Turkey – Turquie
Kültur Yayinlari İs-Türk Ltd. Sti.
Atatürk Bulvari No. 191/Kat. 21
Kavaklidere/Ankara   Tel. 25.07.60
Dolmabahce Cad. No. 29
Besiktas/Istanbul   Tel. 160.71.88
Telex: 43482B

United Kingdom – Royaume-Uni
HMSO
Gen. enquiries   Tel. (071) 873 0011
Postal orders only:
P.O. Box 276, London SW8 5DT
Personal Callers HMSO Bookshop
49 High Holborn, London WC1V 6HB
Telex: 297138   Telefax: 071 873 2000
Branches at: Belfast, Birmingham, Bristol, Edinburgh,
Manchester

United States – États-Unis
OECD Publications and Information Centre
2001 L Street N.W., Suite 700
Washington, D.C. 20036-4910   Tel. (202)785.6323
Telefax: (202)785.0350

Venezuela
Libreria del Este
Avda F. Miranda 52, Aptdo. 60337
Edificio Galipán
Caracas 106   Tel. 951.1705/951.2307/951.1297
Telegram: Libreste Caracas

Yugoslavia – Yougoslavie
Jugoslovenska Knjiga
Knez Mihajlova 2, P.O. Box 36
Beograd   Tel.: (011)621.992
Telex: 12466 jk bgd   Telefax: (011)625.970

Orders and inquiries from countries where Distributors
have not yet been appointed should be sent to: OECD
Publications Service, 2 rue André-Pascal, 75775 Paris
Cedex 16, France.

Les commandes provenant de pays où l'OCDE n'a pas
encore désigné de distributeur devraient être adressées à :
OCDE, Service des Publications, 2, rue André-Pascal,
75775 Paris Cédex 16, France.

75669-4/91

OECD PUBLICATIONS, 2 rue André-Pascal, 75775 PARIS CEDEX 16
PRINTED IN FRANCE
(14 91 03 1) ISBN 92-64-13491-3 - No. 45541 1991